DOUBTING CONSCIENCE

Doubting Conscience

Donne and the Poetry of Moral Argument

DWIGHT CATHCART

Ann Arbor   The University of Michigan Press

For Mary Rinehart Cathcart
in many ways the woman of the poems

Acknowledgments

Friends helped me to make this a better book: Russell Fraser, who knew about Donne and casuistry before I did and who suggested the subject to me and whose support has been a source of warm confidence for most of my professional life; Frank Huntley, whose wit matches Donne's own; Leonard Nathanson, whose care directed my first starts; Robert Stilwell, a poet who cares about prose; and Lincoln Faller, who, like Donne's speaker, knows how complex a subject truth may be.

Prefatory Note

The sixteenth- and seventeenth-century material quoted in the following pages has been modified in these ways: the letter "s" has been standardized according to twentieth-century usage; the letter "i" when used for "j" has been changed to "j"; the usage of the letters "u" and "v" has been standardized; letters referring to marginal citations of authorities have been suppressed. Vagaries in spelling and in punctuation, including Donne's idiosyncratic use of brackets in *Biathanatos,* have been retained.

All references to Donne's poems in the text are to John Donne, *The Poems of John Donne,* 2 vols., edited by H. J. C. Grierson, London, Oxford University Press, 1912. Line numbers in the text are to vol. I of this work. References in the text to Aquinas's *Summa Theologica* are to part, question, and article number. References in the text and the notes to the works of other writers are to the editions cited in the bibliography.

Contents

I

Donne and Casuistry

We do not come to Donne as we come to Shakespeare, whose space and history are in our blood and bones. Donne is surely not all we are and have been; he does not revive the memory of our whole selves. Nor can he render the comfortable assurance that patterns do repeat and that the world may explain itself. The concerns of his poetry are too particular, the approach too special. And, except for those special times when we must resolve our conflict in what we feel to be an hysterical world, we are not at ease with Donne's particularity nor with his tone. In the most of our lives, we think and feel with some degree of clarity and calmness—or think and feel that we do; we express ourselves without resort to paradox. We look on ourselves with disgust at one time or joy at another, but our anxiety is special and we find it mirrored in Donne.

We respond to Donne at those times in life when we must argue, when there is no general assent to truth, when we feel beseiged by generality, when our sense of effects is clear but our sense of causes is fogged by worry and doubt and guilt. Donne, more than other poets, has made it his business to re-create in the lines of the poem that part of life which honest perplexity pervades, in which we are not certain of joy nor sure of horror. The poems represent us not as we love or act or compliment or know or are, but as we argue ourselves out of a dilemma, pulling ourselves out of the mire of the visible world through need and ability and passion. The poems fill us with satisfaction at our success and with astonishment and glee that we are able to assay the impossible. Concerned, as we read Donne, with recti- tude and with the civilized virtues of a sense of order and responsibility—when order may not be real and responsibility unassigned—we feel sophisticated. Sophis- tication is a late accretion to the catalog of human characteristics, and Donne takes us further toward it— forces us to go further in recognizing it—than many poets, and further than perhaps we want to go. Sim- plicity, harmony, and clarity are often more attractive. It is not attractive to contend with enemies, worse to contend with friends, and worst of all to contend with self. But, being self-conscious and civilized, sometimes we must contend to live, and we respond to Donne's poetry because the contention is all there—the reasons for it, the assumptions behind it, the tone that has to be assumed, the method of argument.

This is poetry of argument. The fifty-four lyric poems of Donne's *Songs and Sonets* are, more clearly than any other one collection of poems from the Renaissance, poems whose motive, subject, structure, setting, tone, and premises are those of argument. Donne's speakers use the varieties of logic to defend and finally to sup- port their private and vulnerable views. And one supposes that it is precisely because their views are exposed and vulnerable that the speakers need to argue. Such views derive no strength from indisputable prin- ciples, they receive no general assent; they stand alone as the solitary things they are: one man's often shocking conclusions, and they are allowable only if the speaker of any poem, with his passion and acuity and wit, may convince his listener of their truth.

In "Womans constancy," the speaker says, "against these scapes I could/Dispute, and conquer, if I would" (ll. 14-15), suggesting a tendency in the speaker which is noticeable throughout the collection. This tendency is to "Dispute, and conquer," and it is the "scapes" of the "you" of the poem against which he argues. This person, to a degree, forces him to say the thing he does say—by weeping, by attempting to escape, by putting on a blank face of disbelief, by resisting his sex. This presence of the "you" of the poem suggests an incipient drama to which the poem itself is a response. The dramatic setting of the poems of the collection, articulated to a degree unmatched in the English Renaissance lyric, changes the poetry from the familiar lyric to poetry found heretofore only in the drama. An understanding of the nature and method of the argument, of the conceits and their use, of the function of ideas in the argument, follows on an understanding of the setting out of which the argument arises. The dramatic setting suggests that what interested Donne when he sat down to make a poem was the disagreement between two sophisticated people over ways to act. In poem after poem the issue that divides the two people of the poem is not intellectual but moral. That is, the two are agreed apparently that they must do something and that there is a right thing to do. Yet they disagree on the right course. *Should we weep? Should we have sex?*

The disjunction in this poetry has long been seen— the separation between desire and fulfillment, between wish and fact, between faith and knowledge, between the body and the spirit, between thought and feeling. The sense of the heterogeneity of things is made dramatic by the presence of the "you" to whom the speaker speaks, and the disjunction of the poems begins with the disjunction between these two persons, between the relatively normal and reasonable views of the "you" and the more eccentric view of the speaker. As the speaker argues, he is clearly torn between, on the one hand, a knowledge that his own predicament is special and does not reflect the order of the world, and, on the other, a knowledge that the world order must be reflected in his own special predicament. He is torn between his knowledge of law as an expression of the government of the world and his knowledge of the special nature of his case.

Civilized society has always assented to a system of law, statements of the way in which men and the world do behave. Law is both cause and sign of the harmony and clarity of the visible world. Yet as societies are complex, as the speaker discerns the various behavioral patterns of men and of atoms, he discovers that law—from the law which governs the universe to the codified laws of the community of men—is complex, contradictory, unclear, and frequently inapplicable in the particular instance. And Donne's speaker, wanting to be in harmony with order but stymied because that order is unclear and not reflected in the special situation, needs a particular instrument to clarify the law which he feels governs his actions and to apply that law to his particular case. That instrument is casuistry, and, as the speaker argues with his interlocutor over the moral issue that confronts them, he engages in casuistry.[1]

It is the business of the casuist to join the unique individual to the general law without denying the validity of either. Insofar as the law applies to two men, it denies their individuality, and, insofar as a man insists on his individuality, he denies the world its structure. The anxiety seen in the poems, arising out of Donne's sense of the disjunction between the solitary man and the whole community of the universe, is therefore a civilized anxiety, and the casuists speak freely of it. It proceeds, they say, out of a *doubting conscience,* that is, a conscience wavering between choices of action, and therefore uncertain of law which should govern action. The aim of casuistry—and the aim of the great majority of the *Songs and Sonets*— is the quieting of conscience and the resolution of doubt.[2]

Of course, since faith in ultimate unity of the world is often a religious endeavor, and since Donne's was a religious age, the casuistry we find in his period usually proceeds out of moral theology, the application of law to the particular case of conscience. But casuistry need not be religious. At any time, in any country, when a man sees the disjunction between the one and the many, and when the conflicting claims of self and other prevent action without violence to self or other, casuistry becomes necessary. It is not a body of doctrine, it is a method of reasoning and a habit of thought.

Casuistry asks the question, *What must I do in this case?* A typical example of Protestant English casuistry may be found in William Perkins's *The Whole Treatise of the Cases of Conscience* (1606): "Whether any man especially a Minister, may with good conscience flie in persecution? and if he may flie, when?" Perkins answers by saying that, though some people think that a minister may not "flie," "the truth is, that sometimes it is lawfull to flie, though not alwayes." He shows thereby his bias with respect to the law, and the remainder of the case is the proving of the validity of that bias (the following discussion is taken from Perkins, pp. 215-21).

Perkins first applies to his doubt the scriptural quotation (Matthew 10:23): "When they persecute you in one City, flie into another."

If it be alledged, that if this commandement to flie, then all must flie; I answer againe, that though the commandement be generall to all persons, and therefore every Christian may lawfully shun apparent danger: yet the same is particular in regard of circumstances, of time, and place. For though all may flie, yet there be some places and times wherein man may not use that libertie.

When may one use that "libertie" to flee? Only when certain "objections" are met. These objections are actually laws which seem to deny the validity of the action. The first of these is: "Persecution is a good thing, and that which is good cannot be eschewed." Perkins responds to the objection:

Good things are of two sorts. Some simply good, in, and by themselves; as vertues, and all morall duties; and these are not to be eschewed. Some again are good only in some respects. Of this sort are things indifferent, which be neither commanded nor forbidden, but are good or evill in respect of circumstances. And these may be eschewed, unless we know that they bee good for us. Now, persecution being of this kind, that is to say, not simply good, but onely by accident, may be avoided; because no man can say that it is good or bad for him.

Having considered several of these objections which might be against flight, Perkins then considers those conditions in which flight might be possible. Among the nine which he poses are: if the person does not have sufficient strength for the persecution "after due triall and examination"; "if he be expelled or banished by the Magistrate, though the cause be unjust"; "if the danger be not onely suspected, surmised, and seene a farre off, but certaine and present. Otherwise the Pastor falls into the sinne of Jonah, who fore-casted dangers in his calling, and therefore prevented them by flying to Tarsus."[3]

The kind of argument found here, arising out of a moral uncertainty with respect to an action and referring that action to various laws, is typical of the argument one finds among seventeenth-century casuists. All of them assume a body of law, articulated generally as tripartite, Divine, Natural, Human, and they further assume that man's actions must be in accord with that law. Yet they all, like Perkins, know that law is not perfectly applicable in all cases: "The truth is, that sometimes it is lawfull to flie, though not alwayes." Because that is so, the case of conscience arises and casuistry attempts to bridge that separation between the perfection of the law and the particular case.[4]

Casuistry, as Donne knew it in its most popular form, was religious and post-Reformation. That closest to hand would have been the English Protestant casuistry of which the works of such men as the Puritans William Perkins (1558-1602) and William Ames (1576-1633), the Anglicans Joseph Hall (1575-1656) and Jeremy Taylor (1613-67) were representative. Further afield, but perhaps closer to Donne in temperament, was the Roman Catholic casuistry, primarily Jesuitic and called "post-Tridentine" because its peculiar emphases derived from the decrees of the Council at Trent. Among these writers, the most prominent were the Spanish: Luis Molina (1535-1660), Juan Mariana (1537-1624), Juan Azor (1535-1603), and Escobar y Mendoza (1589-1669).[5] Post-Tridentine casuistry relied heavily upon opinions of authorities to discover the statement of the law, and their books of cases and treatises of moral theology tended to be more complete, more forensic in tone than the English Protestants, who placed faith in the Scripture as a statement of the law and who were more assertive and less argumentative in their cases. But all of them assented to similar beliefs about man's moral duty and his capability of reaching that duty, and they used a similar method of enabling man to do so.[6]

Donne himself wrote an exercise in political casu-
istry, *Pseudo-Martyr,* in which he argued for the neces-
sity of the English Catholics to take the oath of alle-
giance to the English king. In his exercise in religious
casuistry, *Biathanatos,* he argued that suicide is "not so
Naturally Sinne, that it may never be otherwise" (title
page). In these two works, and in the works of the
English and Spanish casuists of the period, the casuist
must frequently defend as moral the immoral act: the
Christian may flee from persecution; murder may be
committed; suicide is not always a sin; the reasonable
man may defend as true a statement which he knows
has little probability of truth. And one discovers strange
things of the reason: truth as it is discovered in the
particular case almost always shocks in the general; one
begins with conclusions of syllogisms and not with
premises; the greater the separation between the law and
the act governed by that law, the greater the probability
that one has discovered the truth about that act; unity is
discovered only in the greatest multiplicity; skepticism
begets faith.

The poems in Donne's *Songs and Sonets* arise out of
the dilemma which faces the casuist. In "The Canoniza-
tion," Donne's speaker is forced to justify the morality
of his love in the face of the conflicting claims of the
affairs of men, and in "A Valediction: forbidding
mourning" he argues, "So let us melt, and make no
noise" (1. 5). *How are we to act?* is the question the
poems attempt to answer, and it defines a case of
conscience. Further, as the speaker applies law to par-
ticular cases, he exhibits the same beliefs about law and
truth as the casuists. His epistemology is the same,
assuming a probability of truth in all law and the possi-
bility of conflict among laws. And, as he believes in a
system of law, in order, he argues toward a moral truth

which is expressive of himself within that order: "Beg from above/A patterne of your love!" "If they be two, they are two so/As stiffe twin compasses are two." Doubt which arises from the conflict between the singular and the generality is here resolved.[7]

The structure of the argument and the assumptions about truth and law and the resolution of doubt are the same in the cases of conscience and in the speaker's words in the *Songs and Sonets*. Yet one recognizes the difference in tone. The casuists are utterly without humor, and the solemnity of their treatises can be deadly, revived to some semblance of life only by a few writers like Jeremy Taylor, whose wit in the great *Ductor Dubitantium* relieves the ponderousness of his concern. One notices again and again the apparent moral blindness of these men who call themselves moral theologians. Wandering in a thicket of distinctions and opinions and probabilities, they show themselves to be indulgent not rigorous, merely legal not virtuous. They show their minds to be pedestrian, incapable of believing that a man may be good or that he may aspire to more than mere legality. One looks in vain through some of these writers for some sense of the spirit; one finds instead endless disquistions on the letter.

Yet finally the effort they make to join man's particular fact to the laws which govern the world mounts in the aggregate to more than empty disquisitions; and, despite the unattractiveness of much of seventeenth-century casuistry, the process of reasoning is not singular to them but accepted by all men insofar as they feel they live in an ordered world and must apply that order to their own lives. When men feel truth is clear, casuistry is unnecessary. But, when men realize that there are after all times when murder is possible and even virtuous, compromises with truth result, sophistication begins, and casuistry becomes essential. It is in that part of life in which, out of frustration, one needs to compromise with the general order of the world, in that late stage of development, that one responds to both the casuist and Donne.

In associating the casuistry of the seventeenth century, both Catholic and Protestant, with the *Songs and Sonets,* one can find a unifying principle that clearly relates the early to the late, the secular to the religious, the skeptical to the committed, the feeling to the thinking, and something that explains to some degree the special response to Donne. One has sensed a unity in Donne, but one has been hard pressed to discover wherein it lay. Since Johnson, critics have been concerned with Donne's yoking of discrete materials, and this emphasis on joining has sometimes suggested that heterogeneity is real and unity merely technical. The conflicting claims of unity and disunity, of gravitational and centrifugal forces in the poems drive one back on the problems of Donne's ideas and their relation to the reality presented in the dramatic setting of the poem.

In the range of Donne's ideas, the reader faces truth as it is manifested in the visible world. The abundance of ideas—the new philosophy and neo-Platonism, science and religion, politics and the church, love of various kinds—has an interest in itself for the reader; few poets seem so catholic in their minds, and the ideas that interest Donne interest the reader. But the further and greater fascination is in that the plenitude and variety of ideas are employed to a common end: the analysis of the morality of an act. Science and philosophy and metaphysics and religion and politics and love all are placed in the service of morality. Donne, like the casuist, is at home, however uncomfortably, in a world which God dominates. The unity of that world, not showing itself, must be proved, and the method of proof is casuistry: the application of law to act and the placing of act within the system of law. The method of casuistry, articulated in the great majority of the *Songs and Sonets,* heals the visibly incoherent world.

The difficulties facing this man are recognized: passion is vitiated in skeptical times, acuity insufficient to dispel the obscurity of a hard world, and wit a weak mainstay. Even when the speaker is able to assume the general stance and argue his listener toward some view which the listener may already hold, the speaker takes the long way about, proving his contention with a method that dismays even while it delights. It is as if he sought to prove to the reader against his will that he is right for wrong reasons. He proves how strange is the world and how peculiar an instrument is the reason. The reader knows he may be mocked. The sense of fun, the verve with which Donne's speaker excites himself and the persons to whom he speaks are astonishing. Yet the undercurrent of immorality is disturbing; there is the slightest hint of corruption, of sin, which hangs over and clouds the gaiety. It has clouded our response to the poems, too, and it has been impossible to locate the speaker's private ironies, directed not toward himself or his world but toward the "you" of the poem and you, the *hypocrite lecteur.* The poet's sincerity is not spoken of here, for many things are legitimate in rhetoric. Yet the poems show an extraordinarily developed sense of decorum, of rectitude, of virtue, and one may deny neither the sense of decorum nor its violation if one is to deal with whole poems and not aspects.

There is always in casuistry the knowledge that the world does not explain itself and that one must force it to be amenable to one's needs. Faith in ultimate unity coexists with knowledge of disparate plenitude. Truth is unitary but formulations of that truth are multiple and contradictory. Truth and its formulation are discrete, and, as the speaker argues himself, his listener, and the reader toward a violent coupling of the two, he violates his sense of the sublime and peaceful order of the world, knowing that particularity contradicts generality. As his truths accrete, as he asserts and proves that round earths have corners, that one and two are equal, out of the strain and intricacy of his argument, the speaker brings himself and the "you" and the reader closer and closer, and more and more triumphantly, to a resolution of the impasse which had paralyzed him.

Casuistry attempts an impossibility, and, insofar as it succeeds, it tends to destroy the reasonableness of law. Yet, in succeeding, casuistry makes a bridge between irrationality and reason, between the interior and the exterior perceptions of truth, between the body and the spirit. Donne's casuistry is a reasonable method of dealing with those matters with which the reason cannot deal: the articulation of paradoxes. It is a bridge between impossibles, and Donne's method is the method of all those who have believed in a structured world but have found an unstructured one, who have felt the possibility of sin, who have doubted therefore, and yet who have felt the need to bridge the several kinds of truth. This method has made it possible for Donne's speaker and for his readers to live with the probability of truth if not the certainty of it.

II

The Dramatic Grounds of Moral Argument

In a great many of these poems one feels that one has walked into the middle of something. "For Godsake hold your tongue, and let me love" is heard upon entering the room; and we sense a conversation in progress, the subject, issues, direction of which become clear only as we listen to the one whose words we hear before we pass out of the room at the other end. "Busie old foole," "I can love both faire and browne," "I am two fooles"—these opening lines have the tone of something said after something else has been said. They do not so much begin a statement as they continue or respond to other statements, and one senses that, as in other conversations, the speaker heard is answering point by point the assertions of a speaker not heard. This person, the "you" of the poem, is distinct from the general reader and from the pronoun "one" and is the particular listener whom the speaker addresses. In some ways the "you" forces the speaker to say what he does say and to some degree shapes the speaker's statement. The "you" is not external to the imaginative creation which is the poem, and the imaginative experience of the poem includes a response to the "you" equally with a response

13

to the flies, the tapers, the eagle and the dove, and the phoenix.[1]

These poems are received as incipient drama. This quality has been widely noted and fully commented upon, and is repeated here because the dramatically presented relationship between the two persons of the poem is the grounds out of which comes the argument of the poems. As the man who speaks and the woman to whom he speaks and their relationship become known, so does the issue to which the poems are addressed and the method of its handling. William Perkins posed the question "Whether any man especially a Minister, may with good conscience flie in persecution"—a question which may have a theoretic interest in Perkins's collection. Persecution is general; the crucifixion of Peter is specific and horrifying, and the question which Perkins poses assumes an importance and an immediacy which it had not had in his book, when that minister has a name and a date and an identifiable persecutor.

The broad outlines of the dramatic element in this poetry have long been clear.[2] Confronted here are two persons—not the more traditional solitary speaker—and these two persons can be identified to some degree. Of course, the man who speaks in one poem is not necessarily the same man who speaks in another, the man who is so lascivious in "The Dreame" is not the same man who speaks in the valediction poems. And the "you" of these poems may be a whore in some or Donne's wife in others. We need not question whether he or she has an historical identity. Donne has many speakers and the speakers speak to many persons, but in any one poem, the speaker and the "you" are arrayed against one another in a familiar pattern.

Usually a woman, the "you" has confronted the "I" of the poems in a way that includes the sexual confrontation but is not limited to the specifically sexual. In some poems, for example, the speaker strongly insists on the unimportance of the physical, and in other poems, the speaker posits the unimportance of anything but the physical. Sex, or love, is of course only part of the meeting of the "you" and the "I" in these poems. These two persons, as found in any particular poem, are capable of confronting one another across the broadest spectrum of human concerns and are capable of defining themselves and each other with a fervor which may excite the flesh but which may also leave it cold.

One has the sense in any one poem of two persons with fine and fully developed intellects, whose interests lie around all the points of the compass and whose experience has been deep and productive. One understands that they know themselves and each other well and may speak elliptically and be understood. One understands that the particular issue which divides them in the poem is only one of many that might have divided them, that it might have been sex, or the sexes, or things which have nothing to do with gender—scorn, steadfastness, selfishness, idealism, cynicism, despair—but not intellect, which never seems to divide them. One knows from the "I" of these poems that if it is only his or her whim that makes them divide on this or that issue, there are other times and other places and other poems in which their positions relative to an issue are reversed. And there are even times and places when the same issue that divided them once will unite them now. If the speaker's mind is catholic, one knows that the mind of the "you" is catholic also, stimulated by all the world's and her and his experience, and in turn stimulating him.[3]

The presence of the "you" in these poems affects the structure of the speaker's statement. In the poem

"The Prohibition," an example of one of the two impor-
tant kinds, one hears "Take heed of loving mee" (l. 1),
and the "you" of the poem is declared with "sighes, and
teares" (1. 4) to be in love with the speaker. But one
senses that the "you" responds after the end of the first
stanza to the words of the first stanza. That response,
the unheard *But if I am not to love, am I to hate?* gives
the speaker motive for the second stanza: "Take heed of
hating mee" (l. 9). Then the silent "you" makes the
logical comment that there is nothing to be done, if one
may neither love nor hate: *then what?* "Yet," the
speaker demurs, "love and hate mee too" (l. 17), appar-
ently smiling. This process is one Donne often follows in
these poems. The speaker apparently changes directions
during the course of the poem because of interruptions
by the "you" which the reader does not hear but which
he is expected to understand. The words printed on the
page, the words read and heard, are of such dramatic
kind and take such directions that there must have been
others, words or actions, both before and after and
during, which are not heard. In a demanding way, this
class of poems forces the reader to respond to a speaker
who is himself in the midst of responding to a speaker.
And, as scientists discover the existence of unseen plan-
ets, the reader must discover the existence and gravita-
tional pull of this unseen and silent "you."[4]

There is another class of poems in which the "you"
does not intrude directly during the course of the poem,
but in which the power and position of the "you" in
respect to the "I" exert a pressure on the manner of the
poetic statement.[5] In "The Legacie," the speaker re-
sponds to a shared experience which is complete before
he begins to speak and which is defined for the "you" in
the first stanza: "When I dyed last, and, Deare, I dye/As
often as from thee I goe" (ll. 1-2), "I can remember yet,

that I/Something did say, and something did bestow"
(ll. 5-6). One discovers during the progress of the poem
that the "legacie," his heart, is missing and that in its
place there is another, "like a heart . . ./It was intire to
none, and few had part" (ll. 17-20). Finally, in the last
line, one discovers that "no man could hold it, for twas
thine" (l. 24). The reader has been held in suspense until
lines fifteen and sixteen before he discovers the nature
of the legacy and why it could not be executed. The
"you," however, has known all the way through the
poem the nature of the legacy. The question for her,
which is implicitly part of the poetic experience for the
reader, is: *Why this recapitulation?* The answer seems to
be that it reminds her of their shared experience, the
past, the frequent coming and going, the gift-giving and
receiving, the passage of time, the simultaneous ease and
distress with which the lovers have accepted absence and
presence. The readers are forced to see her there expli-
citly in the poem and begin to see the poem as a
controlled and gracefully bitter accusation which has
little to do with legacies. The "you" of the poem has
always known that the gift of the heart, the legacy,
could not be given twice, and that what she gave him in
return was no man's goods. A bitter trade. The speaker
has made dramatic for her, her own complicity in his
bitterness. The "Deare," the "you" to which the poem
is addressed, must now see the later bitter statement as
being not merely addressed to her but as being arrived at
or earned by her. The bitterness is not directed toward
her in herself, but toward her in her relation to him, in
her relation to what they have done together; and her
character is less interesting to the poet in itself than in
its impact on the speaker. Out of that impact comes the
assertion of the last lines.

Almost always, the speaker and the "you," by coming together in a variety of ways, create a situation out of which the speaker then makes his statement. In "The good-morrow," "thou, and I" had "suck'd on countrey pleasures, childishly" (l. 3) or "snorted . . . in the seaven sleepers den" (l. 4); and all of it, according to the speaker, was "but a dreame of thee" (l. 7). The greeting he then makes to the woman comes not so much out of himself as out of a commonly experienced past, and she does not merely listen to his greeting; she sees it as part of a continuing dialogue in which this latest statement is less statement than response.

"The Expiration" comes out of present action, the moment of a parting kiss, and it requires that one see the "you" of the poem as participant in the situation of the poem: "Turne thou ghost that way, and let mee turne this,/And let our selves benight our happiest day" (ll.3-4). While it is the speaker who defines the nature of the experience, the "you" is equal creator of that experience with the speaker. The equality of the two people in the closing lines, the reverberation of going and dying—back and forth between them, "going, and bidding" (l. 12)—insist on the participation of the "you" in the experience of the poem. The poem will not allow her to be passive; it requires the active voice, even the imperative: *breake off, turne thou, Goe, ease mee.* The "I" of this poem and the "you" to which it addresses its imperatives are the participants in a small drama of which the poem is statement, complication, climax, and resolution.

It is possible to misinterpret the tone of what the speaker says and to believe that the speaker speaks in some way "down" to his interlocutor, that he has created, or forced, an occasion over which to divide. In such a case, the poem becomes a lecture, mocking or solemn, and not that more intimate thing, an occasion in which two persons converse who have conversed before over matters that have arisen out of their shared lives. They will communicate again, and final truth is never final so long as there is another occasion for conversation. Wit, viewed from this perspective, is optimistic and assured and easy.

But the wit of these poems is not without contention. The speaker characteristically finds himself besieged by the "you" and responds aggressively, picking up his opponent's ideas, agreeing with them in a slanted or partial way, and turning them to his own advantage and purpose. These poems, as they are responses to some silent speaker, show themselves to disagree, even to disagree strongly. There is a sense in these poems of the speaker saying, *No, that is not it at all.* The speaker apparently feels that his listener in opposing him has employed faulty premises, faulty methods, and the poem becomes consequently an attack on the position of the silent partner, an attack mounted out of some greater or less sense of urgency. The passionate and intellectual force of the poem comes not only from the speaker's ability to express in forceful language and metaphor his convictions, but also because the speaker has included within his words oppositions to his own ideas and because the poem is a response to and includes a relatively well-developed and articulated counterposition. No one can disagree with Polonius's precepts. Their opposites are not included in his thoughts, and their force, effectiveness, is rhetorical, not moral or intellectual. Laertes and Ophelia nod. "What a piece of work is a man?" Hamlet asks, and the force of the speech is a result of both the power of the idea, "Paragon of animals," and its opposite, "Quintessence of dust." Equally important, the power of Hamlet's statement derives from its context. The understanding of Hamlet's imagination is broadened and deepened when he is seen set against Rosencrantz and Guildenstern.[6]

This dramatically presented relationship between the "you" and the speaker is characteristic of Donne in the *Songs and Sonets,* and apparently what is characteristic includes most of the best. But it should be noted that, of the fifty-four complete poems in *Songs and Sonets,* twelve are not characteristic, and are closer to the English Renaissance lyric as it is traditionally conceived.[7] The traditional English Renaissance lyric is most often a thinking out loud; and, if the reader overhears, it is a privilege in which he is allowed without embarrassment to enter into a mind which he may admire. Whether the lyric is addressed to someone indicated in the poem or is simply a statement overheard by the reader, the problems of the statement begin and end within the consciousness of the speaker of the lyric; and the resolutions of those problems by the poet are in effect presented to whoever hears the words on the page.

Most of Shakespeare's sonnets to the Young Man, one would suppose, are in this way traditional. Their inception comes from resources within the speaker's imagined life, and, characteristically, they are delivered to the Young Man, not in any real sense derived from him or even shared with him. Their complexity and their power are infused by the older speaker, not demanded by the younger. This is to say that they are more conventional than Donne's, addressed, one suspects, to an idea whose power comes from the poet's or the speaker's understanding of himself and also from the poet's ability to manipulate his language as embodiment of that idea. In Shakespeare's Sonnet 131 to the Dark Lady, "Thou art as tyrannous," the speaker finds himself caught in a paradox (". . . some say that thee behold,/Thy face hath not the power to make love groan" [ll. 5-6]) in which it is difficult for him to judge her without admitting what she has done to him. The conflict of the sonnet is not between her and him but between two opposing ideas he has. The conclusion of the sonnet ("In nothing art thou black save in thy deeds,/And thence this slander, as I think, proceeds" (ll. 13-14) is shaped by his own thought processes, not in any way by her presence. The couplet is judgmental.[8] By contrast, Donne's speaker is argumentative. In most of Jonson's lyrics, the "you," when present at all, is usually present as an object, a receiver, rather than as a subject. In such a great lyric as "Song. To Celia," the person to whom the poem is addressed is merely recipient of the poem. Here the problem at issue—effective compliment—comes out of the speaker's conceptions, and the poetic resolution of this problem in metrics, diction, and image in the lyric remains overheard by or delivered to her, not derived from her. The speaker addresses imperatives to her: "Drinke," "leave a kisse," and turns her responsive action into compliment: "And I will pledge with mine," "And Ile not looke for wine." The intimacy between them, the pleasure the speaker takes in suggesting secrecy—both are subordinated to the compliment he pays her; and saying that she is "merely" the recipient of the compliment means that her presence in no way forces or shapes the poem. She receives it, and it graces her.[9]

Donne's verse is characteristically beyond or beside this tradition. He was not particularly interested in writing this kind of lyric with its relatively greater privacy of conception and utterance. It does not seem very much to have excited Donne's imagination to speak very often only to himself. The lyric is most often a solitary song, and, while Donne can make a song in this solitary mode, he seems most sure of himself, most excited and exciting, when making lyrics expressive of a less private concern. It is Donne's peculiar contribution to our understanding of the lyric.

There are certain pressures a poet feels himself to be under. Among these is the difficulty of statement, that is, the difficulty in creating sequences of images, metaphors, metrical patterns, rhyme, stanzaic patterns, all of which embody his original concept and each of which exerts its influence on all the others. The presence, real or imagined, of a "you" to whom the speaker must respond, and who has disagreed with the speaker before the poem opens, is a pressure special to Donne's lyrics. Those which a more traditional lyric poet may be under in a poem like Shakespeare's Sonnet 65 may be greater or less than Donne's and the achievement consequently greater or less. The distinction made here between the efforts and achievements of Donne and the more traditional lyric poets is not in magnitude but in kind. Shakespeare's speaker, vis-à-vis the Young Man, compliments; and one cannot imagine the Young Man taking seriously the admonition at the end of the poem. What he will take very seriously indeed, one would suppose, is the lyric compliment embodied there in a series of arresting images. Whatever strictures Shakespeare feels on his freedom of poetic statement, and the sonnet form is of course one, he apparently feels no necessity to take the dramatic context into account. The compliment is created by the older man and delivered to the younger. Donne, in a more severely restricted kind of verse, feels that the compliment can best be re-created out of materials implicit in the presence of the "you" and the "I" and which he must handle in a special way. Finally, compliment is in Donne almost always subordinated to admonition.

The dramatic element in Donne's poetry, presented here in synoptic form, suggests the extent and limits of the concerns of the poems. Issues are presented here in their social manifestations, as they apply to two persons; they are not handled in vacuo. The issues of the poems have arisen from the dramatically presented relationship of the two persons of the poem, and the resolutions of those issues in the poems turn back on that relationship, continuing it, changing it. The need for a truth which these poems satisfy is a need which arises out of two people's lives, and as it is so, it has a special intensity. This need is also of a special kind. One man alone may save his soul or give himself up to the last effects of dissolution, but two persons, joined in a common endeavor, depend upon one another for salvation—or for the simplest or the most baroque of pleasures. Donne's speaker, as he seems always to speak out of a shared experience, limits his freedom to think about that experience and the latitude in which he may approach it to the assumptions which he shares with the "you" of the poem and to the changes which he may convince the "you" to make in her response to their lives.

The problems and possibilities of such an understanding are posed strongly by a poem like "A Valediction: of weeping," one of the four poems in the collection whose name defines its situation. In the opening lines the speaker has re-created an image of himself and her and has re-created the sound of his own voice as he speaks: "Let me powre forth/My teares before thy face, whil'st I stay here,/For thy face coines them, and thy stampe they beare,/And by this Mintage they are something worth" (ll. 1-4). Suggesting that he might weep at their parting, the speaker holds back until line seventeen that "she" is weeping, and the reader's knowledge that the "I" might weep tears, "fruits of much griefe," is changed into knowledge that he will weep—if she does not stop. Possibility has become threat, and the understanding of that movement comes from the discovery that she herself is weeping. The power of that threat, gentle and loving, but nevertheless threat, is increased by the three images of lines five through eighteen. If the "you" of the poem continues to weep, the "I" will begin, and the result will be catastrophe: "this world . . . my heaven dissolved so" (l. 18).

The tears which the speaker poses as possibilities at the beginning of the poem were "something worth" because they were stamped with her image, and he recognizes that even her tears are not unworthy since they are fruits, like his, of much grief. But the speaker has pointed out to her in these two stanzas that tears, followed through to logical conclusions, become not simply worthy but even dangerously valuable because they represent too much.

The reader, of course, may feel that the speaker is being hyperbolic in this poem. There seems to be no reason for this excess of weight and importance given to such an ephemeral thing as a tear. At least, there seems to be no reason—until he discovers that she too has been weeping. When the reader discovers that the metaphoric weight the tear must bear is a consequence, an effect, of a condition the speaker has been faced with, then the sense of hyperbole dissolves and actuality remains. It had seemed to be too much, too strained; now, with his attention partially diverted to the "you" of the poem, the reader sees that the intensification of the importance of the tear has come about in response to her tears. The enormous pressure brought to bear by the speaker is resisted by an equal pressure, and, when Donne exploits the metaphor further and further, he seems to be trying not merely to overbear or overpower the "you," but to resist pressure brought to bear by the "you." Force responds to force in this poem, and strength to strength. And hyperbole exists not as an inflation of value decreed by the speaker, but, more naturally, as a result of two persons gradually increasing their estimates of value. As in an auction, the speaker and the silent "you" seem forced to outbid one another.

The hyperbole that is sometimes seen here has no falseness about it. It is not decreed but arrived at, and it is arrived at only through a kind of desperation. All of the dangers the speaker poses are seen by both of them as real, and, as the dangers are real, the responses to them are real too, fulsome recognitions of the tenuous relationship between life and life, and life and death, and virtue and sin. Those responses are so particular that they become unintelligible without seeing her there, responding, reacting, accepting, rejecting, acquiescing, refusing, urging him on to the words on the page. The answer to the question *Why this strain?* becomes easy. The strain is already there "in thine armes" (l. 21). The speaker defines it, refines it, uses it to his own purposes, resists it, with his own strain.

The disagreement over ways to act in this poem points toward the nature of the argument between the "you" and the "I" in these poems. In "A Valediction: of my name, in the window," the situation of the poem, the relation of the "you" and the "I," seems very different from the valediction just discussed, yet the point at issue in the poem is very much the same: The two speakers have not come to an agreement over the way to treat their separation.

The reader does not even discover that the speaker is leaving until the middle of the poem, when he reads that "The rafters of my body, bone/Being still with you, the

Muscle, Sinew, and Veine,/Which tile this house, will come againe" (ll. 28-30), and the beginning of the next stanza, "Till my returne, repaire" (l. 31). The issue between them is not the subject of his departure, for she already knows he is leaving, but the fact that he has left his name carved in a windowpane: "So, since this name was cut/When love and griefe their exaltation had,/No doore 'gainst this names influence shut" (ll. 37-39). Lines nineteen and twenty have hinted that the "you" of the poem has resisted the importance he has given to the carving: "Or, if too hard and deepe/This learning be, for a scratch'd name to teach,/It, as a given deaths head keepe." Lines thirty-seven through thirty-nine show that it is not that the learning is necessarily too hard and deep for a scratched name, but that it is the particular learning the speaker attaches to the name that the "you" finds unfortunate, and against whose influence she wants to shut the window. It will make her "As much more loving, as more sad" (l. 40), he says, reminding her and the reader that her love, while they are separated, is not all it might be, that, indeed, her love for him can survive during his absence only if he has left behind a physical "ragged bony name . . ./My ruinous Anatomie" (ll. 23-24). The name in the window has become not just a keepsake where "you see mee, and I am you" (l. 12), but a guard, a warden, of her morals. Beginning as a parting gift, the name in the window becomes an unwanted insertion into her life, placed there by a man who will not be forgotten. It is an explicit reproach to her, and it is a dissent from her attitude toward their relationship, an attitude which includes the suggestion that the engraving is not only, after all, a name in a window, but also an unwelcome reminder of the speaker's absence, an offensive suggestion that the "you" has less freedom than she might think she has.

The issue between the two interlocutors is over the question *What are we to think about what I have done?* The speaker says, *If what I have done is right, as I think it is, it is right because of some combination of these reasons.* And the poem, part of a partially overheard conversation, is an investigation into those reasons. This poem arises out of a disagreement over an action; and this points toward the most frequent source of Donne's poetry: action, people doing things. The poem arises out of a coming together of two people who disagree over ways to act. Donne's poetic imagination tends to be stimulated by the actions of human beings and by the contradictions of those actions, the paradoxical nature of any moral judgment on those actions. Few other poets are so engaged by the doings of people, few other poets are so fascinated by the implications of those doings. It is from this world that Donne receives his stimulation, and his poetry then is immediate and practical, answering the questions: *What is it we have done?* or, more characteristically, *What shall we do?* He never asks, with Eliot's hysterical woman, *What shall we ever do?* Men, for Donne, are always capable of action, and important action. The fascination for him is in its import.

All four of the "valediction" poems come out of a situation created by two people: his parting and her reaction to it. And in each case her reaction has disagreed with his. "Let me powre forth/My teares before thy face" (ll. 1-2), he says in "A Valediction: of weeping," and all that he says in the next twenty-five lines is an investigation into the implications of that action, concluding that weeping is dangerous and even murderous. "A Valediction: forbidding mourning" is another response to a weeping woman whose "sigh-tempests" cloud the beginning of a separation. Here the speaker, for a variety of reasons, insists that tears in this situation are not wrong but pointless, a response to a separation that does not in fact exist. "A Valediction: of the booke," more clearly than the other three, is directed toward the question: *What are we to do?* "I'll tell thee now (deare Love)," he says, "what thou shalt doe" (1. 1), in his absence: "Study our manuscripts" (1. 10). "Thus vent thy thoughts; abroad I'll studie thee" (1. 55).

What excites Donne's imagination and what produces these poems is the intricacy and the possibility for disagreement arising out of action. *What did we do before?* and *What do we do now that we love?* he asks in "The good-morrow"; and in "Womans constancy" he asks, "Now thou hast lov'd me one whole day,/To morrow when thou leav'st, what wilt thou say?" (ll. 1-2). The issue in "The undertaking" is not whether one may find and love "vertue 'attir'd in woman" (1. 18) but rather, once one has found it, what is one to do? "Keepe that hid," the first and last stanzas reply. Just as the speaker had kept that "hid" and felt a need to justify having done so, he ends his poem with the assertion, "You have done a braver thing/Then all the *Worthies* did" (ll. 25-26), which is to keep that hid. The poem begins in justification of action and looks forward to another action.

Wherever in Donne's mind the poem began, whether in idea or feeling or image, that idea or feeling or image is expressed in its relation to men doing things. Whatever cerebration takes place between the opening and closing lines of the poem is directed toward explaining, investigating, justifying, arguing the implications of active life, an active life in which the "you" has been an

equal participant with the speaker in a very special
private situation. Donne is not a philosophical poet.
That is, the progress of his thought is not directed
toward definition of concept but rather toward direc-
tion of his action. His investigations are not theoretic
but practical, not so much strategic as tactical, not
toward ascetic but toward moral ends. It is necessary to
distinguish between the kinds of thought one may have
about an issue of philosophical importance, and the
kinds of thought one may have about an action. Faced
with completed action, or the necessity to act, Donne's
speaker's mind responds with moral questions.

If we are faced with this situation, the speaker says
in effect, *how are we to act with rectitude?* Because of
this, the poems are always concerned with acting in
accord with some moral law, even if it be only jokingly
believed in or applicable to the two lovers, even if it be
created only to justify the action. The implications of
an action—going to bed, copulating, parting—are always
important to the speaker and his interlocutor. In these
poems there is no act which can be seen as an end in
itself; all lead to something: pleasure, physical or men-
tal; satisfaction; virtue; rectitude; pain. Everything re-
sults in something and every cause has an effect—the
movement of the speaker and his listener, in their dra-
matic setting, closer to virtue.

Such a statement seems deflating when applied to a
poem like "The Sunne Rising," whose gleeful self-satis-
faction, whose facile intelligence are displayed, both
naturally and self-consciously, for all to see, whose
concerns seem to have so very much more to do with
the speaker's concept of her and the world than with his
program for action or concern for virtue. The impor-
tance of the observation arises out of the realization on
the part of the speaker that he may not think and act by

starts, that he is faced with another whose demands on him necessitate that he must simultaneously think and act, that his thought must be toward action and his action thought through. It is not enough to say that Donne is capable of mental and emotional gymnastics. What one must go on to say is that his mind seems to be of the sort which is interested in, is fertile of, primarily the doings of men—but only those doings which require analysis. At that everyday and common confrontation of action and analysis, Donne becomes characteristically Donne. When he thinks, conscious of the intellectual and physical demands which the dramatic situation makes on him, which he makes on himself, which she makes on him, he rises out of mere assertion, goes beyond, or stays this side of, mere ratiocination, and joins everything he knows and she knows to what he is doing and what she is doing. The catalyst for this brilliance is the act: her weeping, his carving a name in a window, the sun rising, her entering a room and waking him from a dream, their transporting themselves in ecstasy. And the catalyst does not remain inert. The action is not mere occasion. The action calls forth pyrotechnics of wit—but fireworks change forever any conception of action. One is forced to believe that the assumptions of the "you" are changed too; if action began it all, action ends it.

And, generally, the action which does end the poem is looked forward to in a series of grand imperatives. The conclusion of "The Sunne Rising" is indicative and is repeated again and again through the collection of poems. "Shine here to us," the speaker says, forcing the participation of the "you," the sun, in the poem and in the action which continues beyond the last line. At the end of "The Canonization," the speaker says, "And thus invoke us; You whom reverend love/Made one anothers hermitage . . . Beg from above/A patterne of your love!" (ll. 37-45). "Weepe me not dead . . ./Let not the winde/ Example finde" (ll. 21-24), in "A Valediction: of weeping"; and "Send me nor this, nor that, t'increase my store,/But swear thou thinkst I love thee, and no more" (ll. 17-18), of "Sonnet. The Token." "A Valediction: forbidding mourning" and "A Valediction: of weeping" are in themselves imperatives not to weep, and the closing third of "The Extasie" is one grand demand not to untie the very human knot that makes us man. These imperatives have the discernible effect of leaving the reader off balance: the command has been given, one waits for execution. The reader is expectant, with some portion of his attention not on the poem but on the response to the poem by the person being addressed.

The "you" who holds the crushed carcass of the flea on her fingernail is just about to speak, the "you" who had been mourning is just about to act, the "you" who interrupted dreams is about to become one; and the deep satisfaction from these poems is a partial result of the sense that beyond the end of the poem, somewhere in the white of the page or of the mind, these people do speak, act, in answer. Partially complete as statements, these poems achieve wholeness in the implicit response of the "you."

The reader of course must provide that response, guided by what he has been told of the "you." The distance between the person to whom the poem is spoken and the reader is wide but not infinite, and the latter's response to the poetic experience includes his under-standing of the spoken as well as the unspoken words supplied by imagination. As the imaginative experience must constantly be renewed, as, with each reading, one must resupply the response of the "you," one is forced back each time into those possibilities of the drama of the poem which never are exhausted, never become actualities. By such means does Donne intimately engage his readers.

III

Truth and the Speaker

When the speaker of the *Songs and Sonets* talks earnestly or frivolously or gaily with a woman, arguing with her over a proper course of action, he attempts to articulate a moral truth. A moral truth may be formulated as *This is the right thing for us to do at this time* and is different in kind from truths expressive of the molecular composition of water or the motion of planets or the movement of ions across the synapses of the brain. The ideas that Donne's speaker holds about truth—what it is, how it is perceived, the end to which it is put—illuminate what he says in the poems of the *Songs and Sonets*. One assumes that all poems attempt to embody some truth and that, as men differ among themselves and are different at different times in their lives, their needs for truth change and the truths they need change. Robert Herrick expresses a truth of sophisticated lyric pleasure when he writes:

> When as in silks my *Julia* goes,
> Then, then (me thinks) how sweetly flowes
> That liquefaction of her clothes.
>   ("Upon Julia's clothes," ll. 1-3)

Shakespeare expresses a very different kind of truth, both more and less complicated, when he writes:

> The expense of spirit in a waste of shame
> Is lust in action, and till action, lust
> Is perjured, murderous, bloody, full of blame,
> Savage, extreme, rude, cruel, not to trust.
> (Sonnet 129, ll. 1-4)

As the truths of these two men differ, their articulation differs, the one descriptive and re-creative, the other assertive and analytic. As the need for truth changes, the truth changes, and the poem changes; and, insofar as the speaker of the *Songs and Sonets* seeks a moral truth, what he attempts to communicate to his listener in the words of the poem and how he must go about communicating it are understood. Epistemology underlies poetic and precedes it.

Escobar, in his compendium of Jesuitic casuistry, *Liber Theologiae Moralis,* asserts a moral truth: "The man who has been justly condemned may not flee from prison" (p. 113).[1] Implicit here and in any moral truth is a law of behavior applicable to all men: *Criminals may not flee prison.* Also implicit here is the existence of a particular person to whom that law applies: *This man has been justly condemned.* The source of the law may be almost anywhere, the Bible, church fathers, canon law, papal bulls, reason, experience; and, as long as the law is clear and applicable, one has no doubt about one's action and consequently no need for casuistry. But the law is frequently unclear or conflicts with other laws, and man is faced with hard questions: "Say that a soldier knows that he is fighting unjustly; may he nevertheless kill a soldier of the enemy army who rushes upon him to kill him?" (p. 118). Casuistry focuses itself upon these hard questions, recognizing that the laws governing unjust wars conflict with those governing defense of one's life and that the applicability of the law may be doubtful. As casuistry seems always to arise out of the hard questions of morality, it seems always to arrive at truths which are essentially paradoxical.

One must make a distinction between two kinds of moral truth. One kind is familiar enough: *Thou shalt do no murder.* The meaning is clear, the authority unquestioned, the applicability to all men decisive. But it is not the kind of truth found in casuistry. Escobar asserts a casuistical truth when he says, "You may kill a highwayman who is rushing upon you not only to defend one gold sovereign, but for the defense of a thing of lesser value" (p. 119). This is a peculiar assertion; it seems to deny the validity of the commandment and to be destructive of our sense of proportion. The moral truths which are asserted in the cases of conscience define *exceptions* to general law.

Escobar asks, "What is prohibited by this commandment, 'Thou shalt not kill'?" and, despite sweeping prohibitions, defines sweeping exceptions: "There must be just cause, public authorization, and the act must be carried out according to the rule of law. The killing of evildoers is not prohibited. The killing of an innocent person is, on the other hand, absolutely prohibited, unless in some instance it is necessary for the good of the commonwealth" (p. 111). This is a movement, quite clearly, for the casuist to justify committing an act that in other circumstances has been known to be a sin. This same movement is found among the English casuists. Bishop Hall, in writing on the case, "Whether, and in what cases, it may be lawful for a man to take away the life of another?" recognizes that sin is not sin in some cases: "If a man will be offering to rob my house, or to take my purse, what may I do in this case? Surely, neither charity nor justice can dissuade me from resisting: the laws of God and man will allow me to defend my own" (p. 397). Hall's willingness to murder in order to defend his own property is foreshadowed in the way the question is put at the beginning: "Whether, *and in what cases,* it may be lawful. . ." (italics added). A glance at the table of contents of *Resolutions and Decisions of Divers Practical Cases of Conscience* is revealing:

Whether, and how far, a man may act towards his own death. Whether it be lawful for Christians, where they find a country possessed by savage Pagans and Infidels, to drive out the native inhabitants; and to seize and enjoy their lands, upon any pretence; and, upon what grounds, it may be lawful so to do. (p. xv)

Each case is directed toward those circumstances when the sin is permissible: *upon what grounds, it may be lawful.* This moral truth, justifying actions which tradition or experience or authority has found unjustifiable, is the moral truth the speaker of the *Songs and Sonets* seeks. Faced with what he sees as hard questions, he seems always to advocate the erstwhile sinful act. He seems aggressively and wittily to separate himself from truths which he had apparently heretofore accepted and from the world which he apparently knows, arguing toward positions which deny his experience and his traditional knowledge. He seems to support truths which everyone knows not to be true and demands the importance of his special case. "Sonnet. The Token" is expressive of this special stance: "Send me some token," he begins, but continues with:

> I beg noe ribbond wrought with thine owne hands,
>   To knit our loves in the fantastick straine
> Of new-toucht youth; nor Ring to shew the stands
>   Of our affection, that as that's round and plaine,
> So should our loves meet in simplicity. (ll. 5-9)

The speaker knows what is generally accepted for tokens; yet he does not want rings and ribbons. It is a more important token he seeks.

The majority of the *Songs and Sonets* exhibits just such a sense of special truth. The speaker's view receives no support from general principles and is in a sense besieged, defenseless except for the cogency of his wit. The poems are not as much investigations as cases for the defense: "For Godsake hold your tongue, and let me love,/Or chide my palsie, or my gout" ("The Canonization," ll. 1-2). The speaker's perception that his love, though profane, is proper, is the motive force behind this poem; and, in "A Valediction: forbidding mourning," "A Valediction: of weeping," and "A Valediction: of the booke," the speaker asserts that he and the "you" must not mourn when they separate, even though he knows and accepts it to be characteristic of human behavior that people apart do mourn. We find him arguing against the experience of human nature in the valediction poems, against received knowledge in "The Flea" or "Communitie," against logic in "Negative love." Most of all, the speaker argues against the "you" of the poem, who apparently represents for him all that is public and all the speaker finds restrictive, destructive of his freedom to act, and repressive of his individuality; in short, the "you" seems to stand for all that is normal.

The "you" in many of these poems has asserted what is orthodox, logical, reasonable, and moral, and, further, what the speaker in other circumstances might have agreed with. The "you" has apparently generalized upon the actions of men, and those generalizations place the speaker in these circumstances strikingly in the wrong. The "you" of "The Canonization" has asserted the worthlessness of the speaker's love in the ordinary affairs of men; Donne's speaker must then argue toward

the special circumstances which make an otherwise irrel-
evant love central to existence. In "The Flea," the
"you" has refused the speaker's promiscuous advance
with the wry assertion that to submit would be "sinne"
and "shame"; the speaker must prove "How little that
which thou deny'st me is" (1.2) in these special circum-
stances. And the tears we discover in the valediction
poems clearly reproach the dry eyes of the speaker, who
must then argue that, in this special case, "let us melt, and
make no noise" ("A Valediction: forbidding mourning,"
1.5). Even the sun, being "Busie," reproaches the lethargy
of the lovers. There is throughout a defensiveness on the
speaker's part which clouds the glitter of his wit, and,
when the speaker seems most aggressive, he attacks to
defend rather than to gain. The poems arise because the
speaker not only is able to defend but feels, with greater
or less solemnity, that he must defend a special truth:
the present virtue of a sin. "Sin" need not be defined.
Men of the early seventeenth century may have thought
the act—whatever it is in the particular poem—to be sin;
but, at the same time, they may not; and it does not
matter, for one does not need to go outside the poem
for definition. Generally the position of the "you," as
recapitulated by the speaker, defines the act to be
sinful.[2]

The speaker's insistence on the special nature of his
case, his insistence that what he is about is no sin, does
not necessarily suggest that the speaker himself is in any
sense special or is in any way predisposed to sin; one
does not after all know how to pursue that question.
One knows that the speaker, sometimes out of an al-
most desperate need and sometimes for the witty and
wicked pleasure of it, proposes to sin and to justify
doing so. One supposes there were times in Bishop Hall's
life and times in Father Escobar's life when they found

themselves in the majority, at ease in a consensus of their fellows. We know that there were times in Donne's life when he felt no need to argue, and when the special case held few attractions. Donne chose in this collection to write poems about those hard questions which also give rise to casuistry—when he saw or forced a disjunction between his own view and the general one. As a result, his poems will astonish even if one ignores the special abilities of the speaker. The truth they drive toward is essentially paradoxical. Paradox denies wholeness and clarity of truth. It denies universality. The defense of the indefensible act emphasizes the heterogeneity of things, the separation of the speaker and the casuist from his fellow men and from the community of the universe. It seems to deny the unitary nature of truth and the power of law to express that truth so that it is clearly applicable in the affairs of men.

For the Middle Ages and for many in the Renaissance and for Donne's speaker also, truth is single, sublime, perfect. "The whole community of the universe," Aquinas had asserted in the *Summa Theologica,* "is governed by the divine reason" (II, 91, 1). Richard Hooker, like all seventeenth-century casuists, Protestant and Catholic, building upon Aquinas's statement of law, says in *Of the Laws of Ecclesiastical Polity,* the "perfection which God is, giveth perfection to that he doth" (p. 150). That perfection, ramifying through all the universe, lies behind visible reality and supports Donne's faith in that "whole community of the universe." It was one whole and, more, it was a reasonable whole, made so by its progression from and its governance by the reasonable mind of God.

This belief in the perfection of God's creation, in the unity of that creation, was for Donne less a result of reason or experience than of faith. Looming large in his religious writings, in the sermons and in the devotions, the expression of this faith in a unitary world is subordinated in the secular poetry to an emphasis on apparent multiplicity, to an emphasis on the difficulties of living in this visible world with all its apparent contradictions: "Yet shee/Will bee/False, ere I come, to two, or three" ("Song [Goe, and catche a falling starre]," ll. 25-27). Yet Donne shows his orthodoxy, his traditionalism, in the manner in which he treats the multiplicity of the visible world. In that world Donne's speaker finds patterns recurring and disjunctions coalescing; he shows repeatedly throughout the *Songs and Sonets* that it is the contradiction between *words* that perplexes—or delights—and that the reality beyond the word is solid and single, often expressed in a drive toward unity between the "you" and the "I." In "A Valediction: forbidding mourning," the line, "Our two soules therefore, which are one" (l. 21), indicates a movement, reinforced throughout the collection: "[we] endure not yet/A breach, but an expansion,/Like gold to ayery thinnesse beate" ("A Valediction: forbidding mourning," ll. 22-24); "If our two loves be one" ("The good-morrow," l. 20); "We two being one" ("The Canonization," l. 24); "So wee shall/Be one" ("Loves infinitenesse," ll. 32-33). The plethora of images in which the lovers signify the whole world is also expressive: "Let us possesse one world, each hath one, and is one" ("The good-morrow," l. 14); "So doth each teare,/Which thee doth weare,/A globe, yea world by that impression grow" ("A Valediction: of weeping," ll. 14-16). Multiplicity in the "two" becomes unity in the "one," and "one" in the lovers becomes expressive of "All." Things signify here as always Donne's acceptance of the unity of the world.

To speak of Donne's speaker's beliefs in a system of law and a subsequent assent to the concept of sin is to speak of an assent to certain beliefs about the manner in which truth functions and the manner in which truth is usable or discoverable. Donne's speaker believes in law because he believes that man's actions may be reduced to formulae. This is a vexed question and it is difficult, if not impossible, to demonstrate what Donne believes. He makes use of such a variety of concepts drawn from so very many areas of Renaissance life that demonstration by extract almost always falsifies. A preponderance of images drawn from one area is almost always negated by images drawn from another area; the medievalism of "Aire and Angels" or "A nocturnal upon S. Lucies day" is contrasted with the modern spirit of "The Flea" or "The Canonization." The past and the present meet so violently and so suddenly in Donne's poetry that one does not know on which side of that great watershed he lies. To what extent, to phrase the problem another way, can Donne be said to *believe* in the conception of geography shown in the lines, ". . . as th'earths inward narrow crooked lanes/Do purge sea waters fretfull salt away" ("The triple Foole," ll. 6-7)? Donne's ideas, from whatever source, tend to assert the predictable behavior of the universe. In any two poems, the predictable behavior of the universe may be contradictory; but in any one poem, the predictable behavior is consistent. The universe may operate in such a way as "no change can invade," or it may exhibit only the law of ceaseless change. In either case, its behavior is predictable, and the speaker of any *one* poem may be said to believe in laws governing the universe. Consequently, there is no need to ascertain whether Donne's speaker believed any one of these concepts. As they function in the poetry, they function the same way and exhibit Donne's speaker's epistemology: truth is that which is expressive of characteristic behavior. And that action which is abnormal becomes for Donne's speaker sinful, or, for the reader, criminal or merely wrong. The poems define these things and one need not go outside them for definition. Generally, it is the position of the "you" of the poem, as recapitulated by the speaker, which defines the particular act to be a sin, and one need not ask whether one also believes the act to be a sin. One knows that Donne's speakers assent to a unified body of truth which functions *as if* God were the author of that truth, and they face the loss of it *as if* it were the loss of the word, which was in the beginning.

This truth expresses itself for the speaker and for most men of the Renaissance as law governing man's actions in the world. Law is a statement of being: "Therefore the very notion of the government of things in God, the ruler of the universe," Aquinas says, "has the nature of a law" (II, 91, 1). "All things therefore," Richard Hooker says, "do work after a sort according to law." This law proceeds from God, whose "being . . . is a kind of law to his working" (p. 150). God's being is God's law, and, when man is created, law becomes a statement of his being as well. Jeremy Taylor, fifty years after Hooker, says that the "law of nature is nothing but the law of God given to mankind for the conservation of his nature and the promotion of his perfective end" (p. 296). Law is descriptive, then, rather than prescriptive; and, insofar as man acts in harmony with the law and his own nature, the law can be defined as statements of the characteristic behavior of men. It describes their *being*.[3]

The traditional Renaissance conception of law had a tripartite structure, the effect of which was to lead to virtue those creatures subject to the law, to "make those, to whom it is given, good, either absolutely or in some particular respect" (II, 92, 1). Good for a creature "consists in its being well subordinated to that by which it is regulated" (II, 92, 1). Law then brings men to virtue by requiring their obedience to law.

The good which results from obedience to law, or the evil which results from disobedience to it, is proportionate to the intention and identity of the lawgiver. The good is either absolute or relative, "for if the intention of the lawgiver is fixed on a true good, which is the common good regulated according to divine justice, it follows that the effect of law is to make men good absolutely" (II, 92, 1). Since God and his Eternal Law are absolute, the virtue which is the effect of the Eternal Law is absolute also. The final result of man's actions in accordance with this law is perfection. On the other hand, if "the intention of the lawgiver is fixed on that which is not good absolutely, but useful or pleasurable to himself, or in opposition to divine justice, then law does not make men good absolutely, but in a relative way, namely, in relation to that particular government" (II, 92, 1). In the same way transgression of the law, or sin, according as it transgresses an absolute or relative law, requires absolute or relative punishment. Insofar as man lives in harmony with the law, he fulfills "a natural inclination to [his] proper act and end" (II, 91, 2) which is his virtue. As one approaches the problem of law in moral theology, one need not concern oneself with whether a particular law is the revealed Eternal Law of God or merely the enacted law of man. As law is true, it describes the characteristic behavior of that which it regulates: "all pleasures fancies bee" ("The good-morrow," l. 5); "What ever dyes, was not mixt equally" ("The good-morrow," l. 19); "virtuous men passe mildly away" ("A Valediction: forbidding mourning," l. 1). The speaker of these poems seeks out those norms, against which to hold up himself and his interlocutor and, in doing so, places both of them within the government of the world in God.

Prior to any moral action the law must be discovered, and the difficulties in that discovery for the doubting conscience are sometimes enormous. The law does not normally show itself; the world order believed in and depended upon by most men of the Renaissance as a statement of their being is not more than hinted at; the law is neither single nor clear and the reason an imperfect instrument. While "Good wee must love, and must hate ill,/For ill is ill, and good good still" ("Communitie," ll. 1-2), good and ill are confused with each other, and one may come to believe that "There are things indifferent" (l. 3), things for whose being there is no law and which consequently are outside the natural order and destructive of it. Law as a statement of being remains as multiple and as contradictory as the visible world. "Many times no reason [is] known to us," even the reasonable Richard Hooker says, and faith in this sublime order of the world does not necessarily lead to a visibly ordered world, much less to knowledge of such a world (p. 153). In a marginal note on a page of *Biathanatos,* Donne says that "first principles in naturall Law are obligatory, but not deductions from thence, and the lower we descend, the weaker they are" (p. 45). This is a weakening of the power of the law in a traditional direction: the law, because it is grounded in truth, must have particular application, but, with each particular application, the universality of the law is perforce compromised. The law itself remains equally binding on all; particular application produces defects.

The law, and the truth of which it is an expression, is known only to a degree by man's reason, both in itself and in its effect. Using the sun as an analogy, Aquinas says that, though we may not look upon the sun, we may see its effects, knowing it only "according to some reflection, greater or less" (II, 93, 2). Every knowledge of truth is a "kind of reflection" (II, 93, 2), and, in that way, "all men know the truth to a certain extent, at least as to the common principles of the natural law. As to the other truths, they partake of the knowledge of truth, some more, some less; and in this respect they know the eternal law in some greater or lesser degree" (II, 93, 2). Ultimate things, for Aquinas, are not amenable to the reason; the totality of the law is something beyond man, just as the mind of God, from which that law proceeds, is beyond the mind of man. Only generally can man, with his reason, discover law and be certain of its relation to truth. Only generally can he be sure of moral rectitude.

The failure of reason to discover truth in its formulation in the law may lead to skepticism, and the skepticism in the *Songs and Sonets* has been widely noted. We have been aware of the speaker's cynicism: "Yet shee/ Will bee/False, ere I come, to two, or three" ("Song [Goe, and catche a falling starre]," ll. 25-27); "against these scapes I could/Dispute, and conquer, if I would,/ Which I abstaine to doe,/For by to morrow, I may thinke so too" ("Womans constancy," ll. 14-17). In these particular poems, the speaker has chosen an easy target for his cynicism: a woman with whom he has no important or enduring relationship. But the cynicism in these poems arises out of a skepticism which colors his argument without regard to the identity of the "you" and which makes difficult the reader's response to the poems.

The speaker of these poems seems able to pick and choose his beliefs, arguing first on one side and then on the other, arguing sometimes solemnly and other times shrilly. He apparently finds it easy to contradict himself and to admit that contradiction does not matter: " 'Tis true, then learne how false, feares bee" ("The Flea," l. 25). He seems skeptical as to the uses of reason as a means of arriving at truth, suggesting that his position is a matter of whim and not the consequence of rigorous logic proceeding from indisputable principles: "For by to morrow, I may thinke so too." Some of the poems suggest that there is no truth and therefore no law; one thing is as good as another: "Chang'd loves are but chang'd sorts of meat" ("Communitie," l. 22). This skepticism is further suggested by the frequency of questions in the collection. "The good-morrow" opens with a question and closes with "If our two loves be one, or, thou and I/Love so alike, that none doe slacken, none can die" (ll. 20-21), with emphasis on the uncertain *if*. Elsewhere we read, "Why dost thou thus,/ Through windowes, and through curtaines call on us?" ("The Sunne rising," ll. 2-3). "When did the heats which my veines fill/Adde one more to the plaguie Bill?" ("The Canonization," ll. 14-15). These questions are sometimes merely rhetorical, but, in the aggregate, mount to more than merely *pro forma* uncertainty: "But O alas, so long, so farre/Our bodies why doe wee forbeare?" ("The Extasie," ll. 49-50). Analysis of any idea or concept, whether religious or political or scientific or scholastic, leads Donne to skepticism, whose speaker apparently cannot locate and prove the truth of a concept. In the sermons, we read, "I need not call in new Philosophy, that denies a settlednesse, an acquiescence in the very body of the Earth, but makes the Earth to move in that place, where we thought the Sunne had moved; I need not that helpe, that the Earth it selfe is in Motion, to prove this, That nothing upon Earth is permanent; The Assertion will stand of it selfe, till some man assigne me some instance, something that

a man may relie upon, and find permanent" (VII, 271).
Nothing upon Earth is permanent, and Donne's speaker
seems left at sea, adrift in the fog of the visible world
with nothing to rely upon but his wit.[4]

This skepticism is found almost everywhere in the
Songs and Sonets, and, as the moral nature of the con-
flict facing the speaker is more clearly seen, the
limits of that skepticism can be more explicitly defined.
The problem facing these two persons is an epistemo-
logical one, and the skepticism with which the speaker
responds to that problem is limited by his faith in the
existence of an ultimate truth. The doubt and confusion
in the poems—and the witty and ironic skepticism aris-
ing out of them—consort with this faith in final truth.
Doubt and faith always went together for religious men
of Donne's age, and the new philosophy calls all in
doubt only within certain severely circumscribed limits.
Montaigne, not the first who did not find a clear and
unitary truth, differs from the speaker of these poems,
whose epistemology seems to be the same as that of the
moral theologians who were Donne's contemporaries.

As the speaker is able to discover truth in its formu-
lation in the law, he does so with his reason, and the
laws he asserts are reasonable ones. In this search for
moral and reasonable law, the speaker recognizes the
consequence of error. The search for moral truth is
therefore made urgent by the speaker's knowledge that
failure to discover law may be not merely an end to a
search but a prologue to punishment. The speaker's
drive toward moral truth in these poems does not lead
simply to intellectual play in which his mind, skepti-
cal of the existence or accessibility of law, abandons
the search in favor of entertainment. In the midst of the
gaiety of so many of the poems, in the midst of the speak-
er's apparent refusal or inability to commit himself

to something he can prove to be true, we sense an awareness of consequences: " 'T'were prophanation of our joyes/To tell the layetie our love" ("A Valediction: forbidding mourning," ll. 7-8). One thing is not finally as good as another, and profanation leads to trivialization and loss. Apparently, Donne's speaker can never in these poems speak frivolously even though he sometimes seems to do so; like the casuist, he is charged with the knowledge of the penalties for not acting with rectitude. The seriousness with which the speaker approaches the issue before him can be seen as early as "Song (Goe, and catche a falling starre)," where the emphasis on the ethical terms in the last line of each stanza, "honest," "true," "false," brings the reader back to earth and insists on the speaker's ethical sense and on the consequence of believing in things which are not true, even the trivial consequence of a wasted trip next door. "The Indifferent" is the first of a series of poems with the same theme, that the greatest hell is to love a false lover:

> . . . alas, Some two or three
> Poore Heretiques in love there bee,
> Which thinke to stablish dangerous constancie.
> But I have told them, since you will be true,
> You shall be true to them, who'are false to you. (ll. 23-27)

The sense of wrongdoing is more acute when contrasted with an instance of virtue, whether "wrongdoing" be constancy or inconstancy in love. It is the consequence of wrongdoing of which Donne's speaker is aware, and he never treats it lightly. There are a right and a wrong; and the speaker, conscious of sin, must make a choice.

What would be the effect of not giving the bodies thanks in "The Extasie"? What would happen if "pure lovers soules" did not "descend/T'affections, and to faculties,/Which sense may reach and apprehend" (ll. 65-67)? The speaker knows: "a great Prince in prison lies" (l. 68). Sin is always a possibility, and the chance that "a great Prince" may remain imprisoned, like the chance that the speaker of "Womans constancy" may "thinke so too" (l. 17), intensifies the problem and raises the stakes in the speaker's search for truth. Like the ghost of Hamlet's father, the speaker of these poems seems aware of tales "whose lightest word/Would harrow up thy soul" (I, v, 15-16).

One does not mean in any poem to force Donne into a particular religious or moral or ethical mold when one says that his speaker is conscious of the punishment for sin. Donne in any poem accepts the truth that men act characteristically and that "laws" of human behavior may be formulated. Donne's speaker seeks moral truth, then, not because he adheres to a historical or religious morality, formulated outside the poem, but because he shows himself throughout the collection to accept a codified system of behavior. Any action contravening that code becomes a "sin" for which punishment is in order. If "Variety" is "Loves sweetest Part" (l. 20), as Venus swears in "The Indifferent," then to "stablish dangerous constancie" (l. 25) is to be heretical and sinful, and the punishment follows: "You shall be true to them, who'are false to you" (l. 27).

We see that the contradictions and the opaqueness of the visible world which so sturdily confronts the speaker do not lead him to abandon his search for moral truth. Donne could never say, as Montaigne says in the *Apology for Raymond Sebond*, "I do nothing but come and go. My judgment does not always go forward; it floats, it strays" (p. 426). Donne's judgment is too much directed by his sense of right and wrong to float and stray. His skepticism is not mere Pyrrhonism. Mon-

taigne says of the Pyrrhonists: "As for the actions of
life, they are of the common fashion in that. They yield
and accommodate themselves to natural inclinations, to
the impulsion and constraint of passions, to the consti-
tutions of laws and customs, and to the tradition of the
arts. . . . They let their common actions be guided by
those things, without any taking sides or judgment"
(p. 374). "Without any taking sides or judgment" could
not be descriptive of Donne, for the stakes throughout his
life are too high. Donne cannot forgo responsibility.
Whether it is loss of love, of the kind of love that Donne
is seeking at the moment, or the loss of his soul, Donne
is aware of the punishment of sin. In "Satire III,"
Donne says of truth:

> Be busie to seeke her, beleeve mee this,
> Hee's not of none, nor worst, that seekes the best.
> To adore, or scorne an image, or protest,
> May all be bad; doubt wisely; in strange way
> To stand inquiring right, is not to stray;
> To sleepe, or runne wrong, is. (ll. 74-79)

To inquire after truth is not wrong; "to sleepe, or runne
wrong, is." Donne never sleeps, and it is hard to find
better explanation for the fervor with which he pursues
the truth in his poetry. He does not wish to stray, and
he knows that not to choose, or to choose unwisely, is
to sleep; and that is to sin. Donne's skepticism is then of
a special kind: it is colored by a moral as well as an
epistemological anxiety, and, as the speaker seeks truth
and as he finds it difficult and sometimes impossible to
find, we sense submerged beneath his gaiety the truth
that one *must* be virtuous.

Specifically, the speaker's skepticism arises out of
the conflict among formulations of law. In a letter
written July 17, 1613, whose addressee is unknown,

Donne says, "Except demonstrations (and perchance there are very few of them) I find nothing without perplexities. I am grown more sensible of it by busying myself a little in the search of the Eastern tongues, where a perpetual perplexity in the words cannot choose but cast a perplexity upon the things. Even the least of our actions suffer and taste thereof" (Gosse, II, 16). This is traditional. How can one discover the truth about a thing if there is a perplexity among words which describe that thing? The casuists face the same kind of perplexity among laws, each one of which is expressive of the truth in the mind of God but all of which, taken together, seem to express no more than confusion among lawmakers.

As it happens, the perplexity about formulations of truth in the *Songs and Sonets* is near the base of the excitement of almost every poem. Donne's speaker makes extraordinary use of the contradictions inherent in language, but this does not lead him finally to a perplexity about things. Ultimate truth, no matter how formulated, remains unitary, and the *whole* of the law is believed—if not proven—to express that unitary truth. One may then exploit the differences among formulations of truth without ever having to admit that there is no truth.

The epistemology of moral theology abandons the necessity for proving an absolute relationship between truth and its formulation, and the moral theologian accepts a probability of truth in the absence of the certainty of it. Two theories, both widely employed by the casuists of the seventeenth century and equally widely criticized then and since, justified this partial separation of truth from its formulation. *Probabilism* and *Probabiliorism* answered questions in those cases where man was uncertain of truth in relation to his moral duty. Man's uncertainty, it was assumed, arose from the uncertainity of the law as it was stated. Laws are not perfect. Consequently, under the theory of *probabilism,* postulated first by Bartolome de Medina, a Dominican of Salamanca, in 1577, *any* opinion of the law was admissible as a statement of the law. Moral rectitude described that act which was in accord with an opinion which had any probability of truth. *Probabilism,* employed largely by the Roman Catholic theologians, recognized that an opinion of what the law was, which was probably true, might not be true, and that any opinion which was probably untrue might be true. One did not know. And, in determining the practical obligation, one settled for that opinion which had some probability of truth, and one did not concern oneself with its *degree* of probability. Escobar, in defining a probable opinion, writes: "A probable opinion is said to be one which relies upon reasons of some importance. Hence at some times just *one* serious authority can serve as a basis for a quite probable opinion; because a man specially given to doctrine will scarcely adhere to just any kind of opinion, unless he has been attracted to it by force of an outstanding or adequate argument" (p. 24). Since an opinion, from no matter what "serious authority," need be only probably true as opposed to being more probably true than some other, it is apparent that the law was increasingly denied its status as a *single* statement of truth. Probabilism relieved one of the necessity for finding the *most* probably true statement of the law. Since it did so, any statement of the law sufficed as a basis for moral action. Casuistry, for the post-Tridentine moral theologian, devolved finally upon a juxtaposition of opinions. These opinions were the authority to which the moral theologians appealed. Less than an appeal to reason, they were most commonly appeals to authority, to Scripture, the pope, the Roman congregations, and the church fathers. Not trusting to the bald statement, the casuists relied most heavily of all on interpretations of approved moral theologians.

Probabiliorism, adhered to by most Protestant theologians, a theory entirely similar to probabilism in its abandonment of the *absolute* relation between truth and formulation, differed only in that the casuist was to search for the *most* probably true statement of the law rather than one with mere probability. As it happens, for the Protestant casuists in England in the later sixteenth and the seventeenth centuries, the law is a practical tool; and, when the casuist gets down to cases of conscience, the law is stated in particular: *"He that lives in sinne, shall dye"* (p. 3), William Ames declares, and states the law as the English considered it useful for ethical questions.

Each casuist seems to have faith that his formulation of the law has some probability of truth. Consequently, like Bishop Hall in his discussion of murder, the casuist has no qualms about disagreeing with other casuists: "But in such a case, according to the opinion of this great Casuist [Lessius], charity to ourselves doth not more arm and enforce our hand, than charity to our neighbour holds it, and binds it up: we may not kill, lest the manslayer, dying in the attempt of this murder, should everlastingly perish. Surely, I cannot but admire this unreasonable mercy in a Father of the Society" (p. 397). Hall finds it easy here to disagree with Lessius, a Jesuit, and in doing so he maintains that he has access to a truth as "true" as that to which Lessius has access. One may even disagree with Scripture. In *Biathanatos,* Donne dismisses the applicability of the commandment "Thou shall not kill" with a passage of tortured reasoning:

But I must have leave to depart from S. *Augustines* opinion here, who thinks that this Commandement is more earnestly bent upon a mans selfe, then upon another; because here is no addition, and in the other, there is, [*Against thy Neighbour;*] for certainely, I am as much forbid . . . to kill my neighbour as my selfe, though none be named. So, as it is within the circuit of the Command, it may also bee within the exceptions thereof. For though the words be generall, *Thou shalt not kill,* we may kill beasts; Magistrates may kill men; and a private man in a just warre, may not onely kill, contrary to the sound of this Commandement, but hee may kill his Father, contrary to another. (p. 165)

He concludes that the commandment does not specifically forbid suicide, and by doing so he shows that he may pick and choose among formulations of the law with the same freedom as his contemporary moral theologians. Donne never states that the law is not in the Scripture. The law as stated in the Scripture is so conflicting, so little made for the precise situation, that its use to decide a case of conscience is limited. Yet Donne uses Scripture. The skepticism here, which is important for the rest of Donne's work and important as an element in casuistry, is of a special kind, and Hall's picking and choosing is an example. The skepticism does not lie in Donne's attitude toward the existence of the truth. Rather it lies in Donne's attitude toward its accessibility for use. Donne has access to experience, the Scriptures, opinions about the Scriptures by the church fathers, each of which is enough authority on which to base a statement of the law. And, since they give to his statement a probability of truth and since probability is all that is possible and all that is necessary, he may act on his statement of the law as if it had an absolute relation to the truth. Only probability is necessary, not certainty; thus, he may with equal conviction act separately on two statements of the law which contradict each other and never, at the same time, deny the validity of either.

In "The Canonization," the disjunction between the two perceptions of truth, that of the speaker and that of the "you," has given rise to the argument of the poem. The speaker never questions the validity of the opinion of the "you" that his love is irrelevant to the affairs of men: "Contemplate, what you will, approve,/So you will let me love" (ll. 8-9). In fact, he agrees so much with the view of the "you" that he asserts his love is *absolutely* innocent of any effect in the affairs of men: "Alas, alas, who's injur'd by my love?" (l. 10). But, to be irrelevant and innocent of effect in the affairs of men is not, in the opinion of the speaker, to be worthless: "Call us what you will, wee are made such by love" (l. 19). And nowhere in the remainder of the poem is the original assertion of the interlocutor ever challenged frontally. *Probabilism* has allowed the speaker to defend his own view without confronting the issue of the truth of his interlocutor's view. Further, *probabilism* has allowed the speaker to defend a view which he knows has *less* probability of truth than his interlocutor's: "all shall approve/Us *Canoniz'd* for Love" (ll. 35-36). The last three stanzas of the poem are a brave and witty argument supportive of that view. *Probabilism,* separating to a degree the union of truth and formulation, frees the doubting conscience to do what it will.

The separation of truth and its formulation in the law is more extreme in the *Songs and Sonets* than in any of the works of Donne's compatriots. He is clearly jesuitical as he supports the virtue of fornication, of lethargy, of cynicism, of inconstancy, of indifference, of usury, of dying—in all its senses. He knows, sometimes solemnly but often gaily—and always wittily—that laws of the behavior of lovers need be no more consistent than lovers themselves. And they need be no more consistent that the laws of God, as they appear to men. *Lovers* exist. *God* exists. And one need not worry, finally, if what one says about the one or the other is bizarre and contradictory.[5]

Jeremy Taylor says, "The very title of the canon law was *Concordantia discordantiarum,* a tying of contradictions together in one string" (pp. xii-xiii). It is an expression of the hard externality of life, an expression of how little truth is amenable to man's powers of reason and investigation. The great faith of Donne and these casuists does not cause them to mince the matter. They accept the conflict of law and, through law, a conflict of truth, this paradox; and, through the casuistry of probable opinions, they feel able to gain access to a practical if not an ultimate truth. It is a ready access, for the faith of these men is large; and it allows them, like Jeremy Taylor, to say, " 'Whatsoever swims upon any water, belongs to this exchequer'; that is, saith S. Austin, *Christianus Domini sui esse intelligit, ubicunque invenerit veritatem,* 'If it be truth, wheresoever it be found, the Christian knows it is his Lord's goods' " (p. xv).

Implicit in the epistemology of these poems is the question of the proper end of man, and the speaker of a poem like "The Canonization" must consider the effect of his obedience to one or the other concept of love. Aquinas had said the good which results from obedience to the law is either absolute or relative depending on whether the intention of the lawgiver is absolute or relative, "for if the intention of the lawgiver is fixed on a true good, which is the common good regulated according to divine justice, it follows that the effect of law is to make men good absolutely" (II, 92, 1). The speaker in

"The Canonization" makes witty use of this distinction by choosing to obey a law directive of ultimate ends, the law of religious love—absolute love—not that of physical or relative love. "Beg from above," he says, "A patterne of your love!" (ll. 44-45); he knows that the law which he fulfills in his love has a supernatural source, not the mere custom of physical love which his interlocutor accuses him of following. The conflict then between the two laws of this poem is a conflict between two goals: physical or spiritual union. And, as Donne asserts the applicability of one law over another because of the goal he seeks, he recognizes that the sin involved in one or another law is relative. Donne accepts one sin, the loss of the "real" world, in order to avoid a much greater sin, the loss of a higher reality: "one anothers hermitage" (l. 38).

The problem facing the speaker of "The Canonization" is the same problem facing the casuist: one does not apparently have a choice between truth and falsehood; rather, one is forced to choose between two possible falsehoods. In reality, this is a choice between two sins. "Thou shalt do no murder" is applicable in all cases except where the exceptional circumstances of suicide are present, in which case murder is of less moment than voluntary suicide. Donne sees that, in those situations that give rise to casuistry, there is no certainty of virtue; he finds in the books of cases life described as a process of choosing among scandals of one kind and another. Forced to the wall by a vicious attacker, the casuist is caught between the sin of refusing to defend oneself and the sin of murder, and Donne's mind boggles at the choice, uncomfortable with the knowledge that, as Perkins says, "though every sinne of itselfe, be mortall, yet all are not equally mortall, but some more some lesse" (p. 21). One is not ever free of sin, and one's life seems to be a process of moving from greater sin to lesser sin. Escobar writes: "Say a woman is prepared to commit suicide to avoid the shame of pregnancy; is it permissible to persuade her to have an abortion? [A] Cardinal de Lugo answers in the affirmative (*On Justice* Vol. 1 ch. 9 sec. 2 quest. 2 #43), if she cannot be diverted from this intention by another means; because this would not be advocating evil, but advising the choice of a lesser evil" (p. 123). "Advising the choice of a lesser evil" makes the casuist uncomfortable because it is so very close to "advocating evil," and it surely must have made Donne uncomfortable at times in his life.

Yet Donne's speaker almost always seizes on just that discomfort as the basis for the satiric mode in the *Songs and Sonets.* At the close of "The Indifferent" Venus says, "You shall be true to them, who'are false to you" (l. 27), with her equivocation between truth and falsehood, each word indicting its opposite. Venus makes the two persons of the poem totter between sins: truth which is falsehood (constancy) and falsehood which is truth (inconstancy). Donne's pleasure, one supposes, at the reader's discomfiture, is triumphant.

Pascal makes a legitimate satire of this aspect of casuistry. In the sixth of the *Provincial Letters,* Pascal presents for the reader a conversation between himself and a member of the Society of Jesus in which the member attempts to explain Escobar's use of *probabilism.* Pascal quotes the Father as saying:

'Popes have excommunicated religious who leave off their habit, and yet our 24 Elders speak like this, p. 704: "On what occasions may a religious leave off his habit without incurring excommunication?" Several are quoted, among others the following: "If he leaves it off for a shameful cause, like going out to steal, or going incognito to places of sin, intending shortly to resume it." So it is obvious that the bulls do not mention such cases.'

I found that hard to believe, and I asked the father to show it to me in the original; and I saw that the chapter in which these words occur is entitled *Practice according to the School of the Society of Jesus. Praxis ex Societatis Jesu Schola,* and I read these words: *"If he leaves off his habit in order to steal, or commit fornication in secret."* And he showed me the same thing in Diana, in these terms: "In order to go incognito to a brothel." "And how is it, Father, that they have been exempted from excommunication on such occasions?"

"Do you not understand?" he said. "Do you not see what a scandal it would be to catch a religious in such conditions wearing his religious habit?" (pp. 89-90)

Apparently Escobar casually assumes that a cleric may fornicate and that, when doing so, he may remove his habit. Of course, in Escobar, fornication is not at issue in the moral judgment. The issue in the question is this: is it a greater sin to fornicate in habit than out of habit? The possibility of clerical fornication has been posed and Pascal's astonished response—as well as the response of the general reader—is to that fact.

Escobar sees the issue as a solemn one: in this situation, does one commit this sin or does one commit that sin? Donne had seen before Pascal the possibilities for wit and humor in Escobar's ignoring the question of whether one should sin at all. Donne would have seen immediately that fornication as a mitigating circumstance makes memorable the conclusion of the case; and, if Escobar was both serious and solemn, Donne knows he need not be either when, in "The Flea," he does the same thing.

When the speaker in "The Flea" begins to argue with his lover, he presses her with a smile; and, as she has resisted him, she appears to be coy, using merely conventional arguments against sex, inviting the speaker to be witty, assertive, ingenious, in destroying her argument. The speaker's tone is casual, playful, wicked, and it is the manner of argument that is at stake, not its outcome. Even before one hears the speaker, it is clear that they have agreed, with smiles, to end between the sheets.

Yet this notion is submerged beneath the point on which they have agreed to divide: *should we have sex?* The speaker suggests, when he says, "Thou know'st that this cannot be said/A sinne, nor shame, nor losse of maidenhead" (ll. 5-6), that the "you" of the poem has taken the accepted view for the purposes of argument, a view easily defensible because it makes silent reference to a system of law: sex outside marriage is illicit. Abstinence is in order. In rebuttal, the speaker asserts the casuistical notion that "Just so much honor, when thou yeeld'st to mee,/Will wast, as this flea's death tooke life from thee" (ll. 26-27). These sides have been drawn before the poem begins, and these two, wittily and by choice, face the same dilemma as Escobar's hapless and incontinent Jesuit. They will sin in this way or they will sin in that way, but sin they will.

The speaker, naturally, chooses to sin in his own way rather than hers, and, when he sees the flea which "suck'd me first" and which is now on the skin of his lover, ideas occur: "In this flea, our two bloods mingled bee" (l. 4). Henceforth, the speaker's argument is founded upon the special circumstances of the flea's bite: "Marke but this flea, and marke in this,/How little that which thou deny'st me is" (ll. 1-2). This is of course very much what Escobar had done—to Pascal's astonishment—in his comments on the occasions when it is permissible for a religious to leave off his habit. Fornication and burglary in themselves have nothing to do with removing habits, but as *occasions* they make the removal of habits necessary. There are occasions when sex is neither sin nor shame, as Escobar presumably knew that there must have been other occasions when the removal of habits was permissible. And, of course, there are implicitly times when the removal of habits and fornication, both of them, are sins. That need not concern the reader; it almost never concerns the speaker. The central point is that the occasion changes the general rule and that, rather than being able to choose between sin and virtue, these lovers choose between sins.

The fine wit of this poem arises in part out of the manner in which the fleabite, as occasion, is employed to justify fornication; the argument over whether to have sex centers around this second and superimposed argument: whether the flea has anything to do with lovers. As we are aware of the drama of the poem, we are aware of her repeated refusals to accept his statement of the analogy between fleabites and sex between lovers, and, in consequence, the speaker repeatedly shifts the application of the fleabite, saying, *This is true, but, if you cannot accept it, then this other thing is true.* The speaker, playing upon the desires of the "you"—including her desire to be played with—poses the successive arguments in such a sequence as to force the "you" into a corner. He maneuvers her first in one direction and then in another, until finally she is caught by her own admission in a certain attitude—the speaker's attitude—toward sex. And the speaker does this by manipulating her in her attitude toward the flea itself. Pascal, wittily and for the purposes of satire, had focused on exactly this part of the argument in Escobar: the casuist's emphasis on occasion had suggested the method for Donne's speaker.

The method is clear: by reference to the flea, the speaker seeks to reduce the argument of the "you," to reduce the importance of sex to the insignificance of the flea's bite: "Marke but this flea, and marke in this,/How little that which thou deny'st me is" (ll. 1-2), suggesting a failure of nerve on the part of the "you." *To do it,* he says, *is a sin, but not to do it is to be a coward.* But the "you," without denying anything the speaker has said, plucks the flea off her arm and prepares to kill it. That their two bloods "mingled bee" in the body of the flea is of no importance to her. The flea's bite is not, for her, applicable to the sex that confronts them, however amusing the analogy may be. Further, the speaker has said of the flea that it "swells with one blood made of two," giving her a way to refuse him. The idea is a sinister one, for she knows that the swelling of the flea is not necessarily "more then wee would doe" (l. 9). They might after all swell more than the flea in getting a child, and she proposes to kill that thought by killing the flea. The analogy is entirely too close.

In line ten she proposes to kill the flea. The speaker's reduction of her argument worked against the speaker, and in consequence he takes another tack: "Oh stay, three lives in one flea spare" (l. 10), beginning the aggrandizement of the flea. The flea is "Where wee almost, yea more than maryed are" (l. 11). We recognize the ploy of his argument. In this stanza the speaker suggests a failure of understanding on the part of the "you." *To do it is to commit mere fornication, you say, yet we in this flea are more than married,* with the submerged notion that to refuse sex at this point after the flea's bite is to refuse what has been sanctioned and even required by the church. The "you" rejects that aggrandizing argument when she kills the flea because sex in the fleabite is for her not equal to the marriage; her murder of the flea is fully in line with her earlier thought that sex itself is unworthy and even sinful, merely physical. That is, she slays the flea to slay his definition of sex.

And, when she does so, the speaker asks, utterly astonished, "Hast thou since/Purpled thy naile, in blood of innocence?/Wherein could this flea guilty bee,/Except in that drop which it suckt from thee?" (ll. 19-22). We know that she has killed the flea, not to suggest the flea guilty of anything but to prove that its drop of blood, stolen from her, is not *she* and that there is no marriage in the body of the flea and no sin in killing three. She still remains after the "murder" and the flea has nothing to do with her. Bites of fleas have nothing to do with her. And finally we are ready for the speaker's response: *of course.*

She is where the speaker had wanted her all along. Sex is nothing: "thou/Find'st not thy selfe, nor mee the weaker now" (ll. 23-24). Sex does not lead to anything, not even to pregnancy. In each forward movement of the poem, the speaker has forced his lover to analyze and accept or reject an analogy of the flea's bite with sex; these analogies have been contradictory: sex is important or it is unimportant, always because the flea's bite is important or unimportant. But what the speaker has not admitted is that, if one accepts the analogy at all, however one accepts the analogy, one will end by accepting the virtue of fornication exactly because each analogy suggests that sex is a lesser sin than some other: cowardice, sacrilege, murder. Like all casuistry, the occasion here justifies the action—however one analyzes the occasion. But of course Donne had, like Pascal, seen the intrinsic wit of using a flea, like fornication, to justify acts which might not otherwise have been justifiable.

One can imagine the speaker's lover responding to these twenty-seven lines with laughter and shared pleasure. It is worth pointing out the extent to which the woman in this poem has helped to create the poem. As in so many other poems of the *Songs and Sonets,* this woman has, through her wit, established the context within which the speaker entertains her. She has given him a point against which to argue and then she has not given in to him until he has shown her that she must. She might, of course, simply have acquiesced after the first stanza; surely she plans to do so in the end anyway. But her preparing to kill the flea in line ten signifies to the speaker that he will not easily get his way. She forces him on and on, and, as she does so, she signifies that what will happen after the end of the poem will not be *his way* but *their way,* in which wit is not merely preparatory to sex. For these two, sex without wit is nothing at all.

A habit can be removed for fornication or burglary; sex is permissible in the special circumstances of the flea's bite. In neither case is the circumstance itself open to analysis. That is, neither the possible virtue of fornication nor the applicability and importance of the flea's bite are at issue. Both are merely circumstances which, if present, change the general rule. And at least part of the delight and astonishment with "The Flea" arises from the same source as Pascal's delight with Escobar's argument: as one has found memorable Escobar's justification-by-fornication, here in "The Flea" the reader finds memorable Donne's justification-by-flea-bite.

Casuistry has had the reputation of proving *Whether and on what occasions one can murder one's neighbor,* and the casuists seem to find it easy to discover that sometimes it would be a greater sin to let one's neighbor live than to murder the man. Donne's speaker seizes on the opportunity in this collection, asserting the present virtue of erstwhile sins by suggesting the possibility of a greater sin, and he makes more pointed the wit of his argument by making the justification the more spectacular. Most of Donne's poems argue in this manner. In at least three of the valediction poems, "The Canonization," "The good-morrow," and others, the speaker argues toward his point by asserting that he and the "you" face not one but a variety of scandals, and the most scandalous of all is a denial of their love, sacrosanct and inviolable.

The law presupposes the existence of another kind of truth, different from "the law," and arising out of a different source. The doubting conscience must have a sense of himself, independent of the law, which he may bring to the law. It is a sense of what he is, of his situation, of his will to act. As the casuist recognizes these personal and intimate truths, he gives his assent to two separate and sometimes discrete perceptions of what is ultimately the same truth. Such an assent is exhibited in "The good-morrow," though the sense of argument is perhaps more restrained than elsewhere in the collection. The speaker states his purpose in the beginning of the second stanza: "And now good morrow to our waking soules" (l. 8); and the poem itself is an elaborate "good morning," formal, graceful, tender. Yet there are curious lines in the poem: "Which watch not one another out of feare" (l. 9). Why is it even a possibility that these two lovers, waking into the daylight, might "watch . . . one another out of feare"? Why has he suggested that prior pleasures were engaged in "childishly" (l. 3)? "Were we not wean'd till then" (l. 2) . . . Or snorted we in the seaven sleepers den?" (l. 4). Why should it be that love "all love of other sights controules" (l. 10)? Why is there here the assertion that their hemispheres exist "without sharpe North, without declining West" (l. 18)? And, finally, why does the speaker feel compelled to use the subjunctive in the last two lines: "If our two loves be one, or, thou and I/Love so alike, that none doe slacken, none can die" (ll. 20-21)? And, in a "good morning," why must the speaker close his greeting with that last word: *die*?

The pasts of these two persons seem to close in on them, and the rest of the world seems to reduce the compass of their own, the bed in which they lie, and the certainty of death makes impossible the permanence of their love. When the speaker begins to speak, saying, "I Wonder by my troth, what thou, and I/Did, till we lov'd?" (l. 1-2), the emphasis is equally on "lov'd" and the "we" that precedes it, a notion supported four lines later: "If ever any beauty I did see,/Which I desir'd, and got, t'was but a dreame of thee" (ll. 6-7). The speaker is clearly aware of the pleasures and the beauty which he had desired and got before he desired and got this present pleasure and beauty; and he is aware of the pleasures the two of them experienced before they loved. He feels the need to separate himself from the past to celebrate the present. Fear, his past, their past, the outer world, death—all these complicate his graceful "good morning" and are expressions of a truth which coexists with and limits the truth of his love. One truth, of course, lies in such lines as "And makes one little roome, an every where" (l. 11); but other truths, which other men may share, are suggested in the constant references to "other sights" (l. 10), "new worlds" (l. 12), "sharpe North" (l. 18), "declining West" (l. 18), "slacken" (l. 21), "die" (l. 21). Even waking to a warm sun in a warm bed, the speaker cannot forget other pleasures, other fears, other worlds, and the compliment he pays her in the poem is paid in the face of other knowledges. He asserts a truth he knows has no general assent and no general support in experience. Of course, there is always the possibility that the reader, hearing the speaker assert the validity of his love, may respond with easy agreement. Outside the world of the poem, love frequently avails, finding itself alone and conquering on the field of one's life. But within this poem love is permanent and important only in the face of an opposition which the speaker recognizes to be generally true although not applicable here and now.

While this poem suggests the pattern, it is relatively unusual in that the position which the speaker must counter is one that he himself brings forward. The "you" of this poem appears to be merely listener. "Breake of day" is more characteristic. The "you" of that poem has asserted, apparently, a truth which has placed the speaker in the position of sinning and which has conflicted with the speaker's private assumptions. Here, the speaker, a woman, answers the statements made by a male "you":

> 'Tis true, 'tis day; what though it be?
> O wilt thou therefore rise from me?
> Why should we rise, because 'tis light?
> Did we lie downe, because 'twas night? (ll. 1-4)

The "you" has taken the commonsense line that, it being daylight, it is time to get out of bed. The speaker asserts that mere daylight has nothing to do with lying down or with rising.

This double assent to truth is grounded in the way that man, for the Middle Ages and the Renaissance, participated in truth. As Aquinas demonstrates, man, a reasonable creature, understands the law with his reason and actively imposes it on himself and on others. By this active participation in the Eternal Law, "[man] has a share of the eternal reason, whereby [he] has a natural inclination to [his] proper act and end; and this participation of the Eternal Law in the rational creature is called the natural law" (II, 91, 2). Here the same truth—expressed as God's Eternal Law governing the behavior of the created universe—operates and is perceived in two discrete ways: one's intuited knowledge of one's own "proper act and end," on the one hand, and, on the other, one's reasoned discovery of the natural law which governs that "proper act and end." In one's relation to the law, one is both creator and created, imposing actively the law on oneself and passively receiving the stricture of that law.

Definitions of conscience in the works of the English casuists accept and explain this double perception of truth. William Perkins says of conscience: "For it signifieth a knowledge joyned with a knowledge and it is so tearmed in two respects. First when a man knowes or thinkes any thing, by meanes of Conscience, he knowes what he knowes and thinkes. Secondly, because by it man knowes that thing of himselfe, which God also knowes of him. Man hath two witnesses of his thoughts, God, and his owne Conscience: God is the first and chiefest; and Conscience is the second subordinate unto God, bearing witnes unto God either with the man, or against him" (p. 26).[6] Ames further defines these two "knowledges" in the following way: "Gods Commandement and mans fact are mutually joyned together, and as it were linked with man, whilst both passe sentence on him" (p. 19). William Ames exhibits the relationship between the two perceptions of truth in the following syllogism:

> *He that lives in sinne, shall dye:*
> *I live in sinne:*
> Therefore, *I shall dye.* (p. 3)

As it happens in most cases of conscience, however, the minor premise is less often a statement of simple fact than it is a statement of a paradox: *I kill but I do no murder.* The private perception of truth of the doubting conscience, deriving from an intuition of itself, is rarely capable of rational analysis, for it does not derive from the reason and is not expressed in reasonable language. The doubting conscience senses something of himself which his reason and the reasonable law state to be untrue: *I am virtuous despite the law.*

Joining these two perceptions of truth is the business of casuistry, and it is the same "business" we find in Donne's poems. "Mans fact"—the speaker's conception of his predicament—is joined to "Gods Commandement"—the external judgment of the "you." The speaker and the "you" have to deal not only with the public and universal truths of the "you" but also with the private perceptions welling up from within the recesses of the mind of the speaker. The "you" of "A Valediction: forbidding mourning" finds separation a cause of grief; the visible separation of bodies is an end to union for her. His removal of himself is a removal of eyes, lips, hands; and, as she loved those eyes, lips, and hands, his leaving is destructive to love. They *are* sublunary lovers, she knows. Yet the speaker has perceived the same love in a different way: "Our two soules therefore, which are one,/Though I must goe, endure not yet/A breach" (ll. 21-23), a truth nowhere provable in experience or in logic and without the authority of received knowledge. In poem after poem, the speaker asserts as true a conception of themselves which derives from sources other than the reason and a conception incapable of rational analysis: "Since thou and I sigh one anothers breath,/Who e'r sighes most, is cruellest, and hasts the others death" ("A Valediction: of weeping," ll. 26-27). The identity between the two lovers, asserted here, the mirrored reflection of each lover in the other, for he is both himself and her and she is both herself and him, is a paradox and leads to the further paradox: *as we weep, we kill ourselves.* That paradox confronts harshly the very reasonable truth of the "you": *we love, we separate, we weep.* As these two truths are different in their source, the one from the reason, the other from the intuition, they differ in the form of their articulation. The law is formulated as a declarative sentence defining action. The speaker's private truth, on the other hand, is formulated as a logical paradox. As these two perceptions of truth are joined together a union of man's fact with God's commandment becomes a union of feeling and understanding. The speaker feels his truth to be right; he attempts to understand that it is right. He attempts to formulate his paradoxical truth in such a way as he and his interlocutor may understand it with their reason. As the speaker succeeds in joining these separate expressions of truth, he arrives at a knowledge of the "government of things in God" and surmounts the failure of reason to deal with the multiplicity of the visible world, joining himself to clear and final truth.

This may help to explain the obvious equality between the speaker and the "you" of these poems. One almost never has the sense that the "you" has been merely rejected in the argument; she has been accepted and answered, and her statements made before the poem itself begins are given all the serious attention which the casuist gives to received opinion—to God's commandment. The speaker knows that she is, after all, in touch with the reticulated pattern of the world, that she is in harmony with the idea in the mind of God. The speaker knows that it is *he* who is eccentric. It is not merely a compliment that he pays her when he speaks to her without condescension. She represents in these poems order and reason and continuity and consistency, and the speaker knows he may not remain forever an anomaly. Neither Donne nor the casuist is willing to assert the sole authority of the irrational, private intuition, for that becomes an acceptance merely of one man's eccentric opinion. Neither are they willing to accept as final the authority of imposed law, for that makes man merely a cog in a legal machine. The movement of the poems is toward union of the two perceptions of truth, toward a bridge between the speaker's own notion and a publicly accepted notion. We see "The Flea" as a connection between these two kinds of truth and as a working out of the relation between the "you," purpling her "naile, in blood of innocence" (l. 20), and the "I," asserting, "Just so much honor, when thou yeeld'st to mee,/Will wast" (ll. 26-27). The relation may be between the spiritual and the physical; that, after all, is what Ames meant when he said that, in the conscience, "Gods Commandement and mans fact are mutually joyned together." There is of course no real disjunction between the physical and the spiritual; the disjunction dissolves in the mind of God. But, as the world appears, the disjunction grows to great magnitude and becomes critical in man's search for moral truth.

"If it be truth," Taylor asserted, the believer will know it; yet casuistry arises, and the speaker begins to speak precisely because the "Lord's goods" are not immediately recognizable. Each time, in each special case, he must begin all over to search for and to define his truth. In no poem is this more true than in "The Extasie," whose very title seems to refer to an extraordinary way of knowing. Perhaps epistemology is even its subject:

> If any, so by love refin'd,
>   That he soules language understood,
> And by good love were growen all minde,
>   Within convenient distance stood,
> He (though he knew not which soule spake,
>   Because both meant, both spake the same)
> Might thence a new concoction take,
>   And part farre purer then he came. (ll. 21-28)

The speaker here is clearly concerned with showing that he has become "all minde" and that only by becoming so pure may he or anyone understand the truth expressed in "soules language." It is "by love refin'd," "by good love"—by these ways of knowing—that one comes to the knowledge of this "new concoction" which "doth unperplex/(We said) and tell us what we love" (ll. 29-30). The speaker then attempts a definition of that truth, concluding with easy assurance, "Wee then, who are this new soule, know,/Of what we are compos'd, and made" (ll. 45-46). *How we know* and *What we know* are two concerns of the poem, perhaps even the two major concerns, and the poem seems to be an assay at an epistemology for lovers. The "argument" over "The Extasie," whose history Helen Gardner has defined, may have resulted from a misunderstanding of the epistemology of the poem. The kind of truth the speaker seeks, and his necessary method of arriving at that truth may not have been recognized.

How we know for these two persons, at least in the first forty-eight lines, is by ways other than the rational. It is through a process of refinement of the soul as it purifies itself of the body: "Our soules, (which to advance their state,/Were gone out,) hung 'twixt her, and mee" (ll. 15-16). The precondition for knowing is just this going out of the soul from the body, and it becomes not merely prerequisite but method: "Wee see *by this,* it was not sexe" (l. 31; italics added). Even more clearly are the first forty-eight lines of the poem a definition of *What we know.* As the two lovers sit on the pregnant bank, they seek to "make us one" (l. 10), and what they learn in the ecstasy makes them one, even in their language: "Because both meant, both spake the same" (l. 26). The knowledge that they seek and that surely the speaker seeks is not knowledge of her or of him, not sex, not "what did move" (l. 32), but knowledge of what it is they create when they come together, a "new concoction" (l. 27), "Mixture of things" (l. 34), "That abler soule" (l. 43). It is a truth which is not grounded in any sensory experience; it is a truth out of two separate persons translated into a new soul "whom no change can invade" (l. 48). Nowhere is that truth which defines them in the ecstatic state related in any way to the world of the senses. What they know of themselves in these forty-eight lines is of themselves as they have "growen all minde" (l. 23).

The truth of the ecstatic state toward which they drive is not a truth which may be employed, and the poem as it stands down through line forty-eight is not didactic. These lines do not look beyond themselves and as truth have nothing to do with the affairs of men. They illuminate and purify but to no practical end; the force of the truth is not centrifugal but gravitational. Like mystical truth generally, the truth of the ecstasy seems to be inward looking and useless in application. If one must return from the ecstatic state, one can bring back with one only the memory of that truth, not the thing itself, and only by changing it can one make it change one's life. The effect of attaining such a truth is inevitably to be drawn back again and again deeper and deeper into the ecstatic state where alone the truth has validity. This mystical truth makes all else seem sepulchrous like the bodies on that bank, and its brilliance throws all else into deep shadows of insignificance. With its own special intensity, it makes other truths weak and denies the validity of other values. For those two on that pregnant bank, there seems for a time to be no other life but what they create invisibly between them.

Yet, as the poem seems to shift its emphasis and focus after line forty-eight, it refers to two separate and distinct needs for truth, the spiritual and the physical, and the truths defined in the poem seem to be of separate and contradictory things. The first forty-eight lines of the poem describe one thing and the final lines argue toward another, and the relation between the two remains unclear. The question in lines forty-nine and fifty amazes, and the last lines of the poem seem anti-climactic, a falling away at best, and, at worst, immoral. It is not immediately known what it is in the speaker's situation that has made the discovery of some new truth essential, nor is it known what kind of truth is wanted. The speaker, before the poem opens, is faced with the fact of the ecstasy, and the truth about that fact is undeniable. Insofar as his interlocutor has experienced the ecstasy with the speaker, the truth is demonstrable and proven. Yet that truth is not fully expressive of his situation, as opposed to the situation they share, because he has already drawn back from the ecstasy enough to cogitate upon it and to describe it and to be aware of other truths. The truths of the ecstatic state are clear; but other truths are suggested in the first forty-eight lines; and, as they more and more clearly bear upon the speaker's consciousness, these other truths overbear the speaker's awareness of the ecstasy itself and drive him toward subjects and formulations which link him, in the end, with the speakers of the other poems of the *Songs and Sonets*. This speaker, like the others, seeks a moral truth.[7]

The tenses of the verbs in the first section of the poem support our understanding that, as the speaker begins, he describes a fact which has existed in perfect articulation before one becomes aware of the sound of his voice. The first twenty-eight lines are in the past tense; and, when the speaker shifts to the present, "This Extasie doth unperplex" (l. 29), his meaning is clear, for he shows the tense of the observation with "(We said)" (l. 30). This is followed by a series of past and present tenses set in antithesis to one another: "Wee see by this, it was not sexe,/Wee see, we saw not what did move" (ll. 31-32). As he more and more explicitly establishes that *this was what we saw then,* our ignorance of *what we see now* becomes more palpable. Past achievements have led him into present difficulties. The speaker began to speak in line one not to describe the ecstatic state or to investigate what it is they do, still less to employ his knowledge of ecstasy to some base purpose, but to confront the issue of the future, which may or may not continue the ecstasy of the first forty-eight lines.

The need to confront the future is made more urgent by the bodies of the two lovers, lying abandoned on the bank. Through line twelve, the speaker had set the scene, and he did so by describing the bodies and the postures of the two lovers on a bank. But beginning with line thirteen, the speaker describes the souls:

> As 'twixt two equall Armies, Fate
>   Suspends uncertaine victorie,
> Our soules, (which to advance their state,
>   Were gone out,) hung 'twixt her, and mee. (ll. 13-16)

From this point down through line forty-eight, the

emphasis is on the souls' union as separate from the bodies, which are like "sepulchrall statues" (l. 18). From line eighteen to line forty-eight, the speaker does not mention the bodies of the two lovers; yet the reader, and later one finds the speaker also, is aware of them. There is no feeling of completeness about this middle section, despite the description of perfect union. The bodies are still there. This claim of the bodies on the souls is the second determining factor in the speaker's situation. The poem, had it ended with line forty-eight and had the bodies been less prominent in the opening lines, could have been a re-creation in verse of what it was they were on that bank, as opposed to what it was they did on that bank. Yet the separation from bodies is not yet total, and the speaker, seeing himself as acting in time and in the physical world, in short, as a man with a body, must make some decision with respect to that body, even if it is to make complete the separation between souls and bodies.

The most perplexing aspects of the first forty-eight lines of the poem are those which have to do with the speaker's awareness of other men. Twice in the poem, after line twenty-one and in the closing eight lines of the poem, the speaker refers to others who are surely imaginary, merely posited, but who as surely are somehow necessary to the speaker's existence and to his experience of the ecstasy. In such a setting, "Where, like a pillow on a bed,/A Pregnant banke swel'd up" (ll. 1-2), with its undercurrent of sexuality, the speaker's insistence that someone might have "within convenient distance stood" (l. 24) seems peculiar at best and may be worse. Yet it seems possible to understand why the speaker thinks of other men at a time like this and to apprehend the effect of his thought on the course of the poem.

Through line twenty the speaker has described the two of them lying silently and motionless on that bank:

> Wee like sepulchrall statues lay;
> All day, the same our postures were,
> And wee said nothing, all the day. (ll. 18-20)

In the next line the speaker says, "If any, so by love refin'd," introducing the imagined observer, in part, to bridge the chasm between the lovers' silent and invisible experience on the bank and the words which the speaker articulates and which appear on the page. The motionless and wordless ecstasy is not understandable in any reasonable sense unless the speaker may make clear that to have "growen all minde" is not to have gotten beyond all language. In fact, as the imagined observer understands "soules language" he suggests at this relatively early stage of the poem the nature of the communication between the lovers: "Because both meant, both spake the same" (l. 26), and what they mean is the "new concoction" which can in fact be understood through language and the mind. Immediately after this suggestion the speaker begins his full analysis of what they do there on that bank: "This Extasie doth unperplex" (l. 29). In short, as the speaker senses the need to verbalize and to analyze the ecstasy in more than "soules language," he refers to an outsider who, perhaps, within his mind, is going through the same mental processes. The imagined observer is, in part, a transitional device moving the speaker from the silence and stillness of the earlier portions of the poem to the mental activity of the middle and later portions of the poem.

This imagined observer is further described as parting "farre purer then he came" (l. 28), a suggestion implying that the ecstatic state may be reached not only through the personal process of the soul's release from the body but also through example. Purity may be achieved through observation as well as through refinement. The lovers, having become mystics and therefore separate from the affairs of men, at the same time become teachers and consequently are inextricably involved in the affairs of men. They are not merely a "new concoction" by "love refin'd," but, in fact, love revealed, not to each other but to the world in the person of this imagined observer. The fact of the ecstasy ramifies beyond themselves into the affairs of men.

Despite the fact that the imagined observer has "growen all minde" (l. 23) and "soules language understood" (l. 22), the observer experiences the lovers' ecstasy through his senses. The "soules language" is verbal only on the page of the book and consequently unheard; but the ecstasy they share between them on that bank is sensory to the point that it may be seen, at least by those who understand "soules language." This observer, parting from the scene on that bank, goes away with a heightened and renewed awareness of the possibilities for love. As he parts far purer, he defines for the speaker and his lover an aspect of their ecstasy that their physical immobility had not before suggested: "soules language," like light, may transform that on which it shines without itself being other than what it simply is.

The lovers exist in a pattern of human relationships, and there is strongly here the suggestion that men are not alone and that, as they achieve truth for themselves, they achieve a truth which may be understood fully only as they make reference to other men. Further, as they achieve truth, they achieve a truth which can only be fully realized as it applies. The private perceptions of "what we love" not only must be made public, but are in fact public, in their essence. Like the lovers in "The Canonization," the lovers in "The Extasie" must see themselves as a "patterne."

The need which the speaker has experienced and which the poem itself satisfies is not a need to investigate or analyze or describe the ecstasy itself. The truth of the ecstasy has already been achieved and defined in retrospect in the first forty-eight lines of the poem. But, as the bodies, the present, the imagined observers weigh upon the speaker, that truth becomes insufficient. The need for a decision arises out of the conflicting claims upon the speaker of a variety of truths, and the speaker knows that there is a disjunction between, on the one hand, his intuition of himself and of his private state, and, on the other, these truths perceived rationally. None of these truths, taken alone, is identical with his private perception of himself.

The speaker needs to unite his sense of himself which arises out of private intuition with the varieties of other truths stated or suggested within the poem. And, as he does so, he must make his sense of himself identical with the aggregate of every other perception of truth. He may, of course, deny those other truths and sever himself from the community of men, denying their claim upon him, and from the bodies which are mere "spheres," and which are not "wee." And he may ignore the possibilities of the present, bringing the past, the ecstasy, into the present unchanged, stable, eternal. But to do so is to assert that men live in such a manner as "no change can invade"; it is also to assert that there is no necessary connection between the body and the soul or between person and person. To deny these claims is to assert that they are not "true" claims, for they conflict with prior claims, and the speaker knows that one denies the truth of a statement only at one's peril. All statements have some probability of truth. The problems incident upon his need for a decision are increased by his epistemology: he may not simply deny the validity of other truths; he must recognize these claims as valid and as having some probability of truth.

The bridging of these truths is the business of the last section of the poem and is stated most explicitly in these famous lines:

> As our blood labours to beget
>   Spirits, as like soules as it can,
> Because such fingers need to knit
>   That subtile knot, which makes us man:
> So must pure lovers soules descend
>   T'affections, and to faculties,
> Which sense may reach and apprehend,
>   Else a great Prince in prison lies. (ll. 61-68)

It is the union of the physical and the spiritual which is "that subtile knot," and without that knot man is not fully man; the soul, divorced from the body which gives it freedom to act, is a great prince imprisoned. The speaker further asserts,

> To'our bodies turne wee then, that so
>   Weake men on love reveal'd may looke;
> Loves mysteries in soules doe grow,
>   But yet the body is his booke. (ll. 69-72)

That which makes him man also places him within the community of men, and what he is, is perforce revealed. The poem argues toward a condition in which man must love and must be fully human within a society of humans—all at the same time.[8]

It is only through action that the speaker's private truth of himself may be upheld along with the more public truths which unite the speaker and his lover with their bodies and with the community of men, for it is only through action that man places himself within the public order. Consequently, the poem satisfies a need for a moral truth, a truth which will be expressive of the union of body and soul, of the intimate and inextricable relationship among men, of the relationship between act and law as expressive of the unity of the world.

The kind of truth which has been at issue in the *Songs and Sonets* has seldom been a mystical truth, separate from the ordinary affairs of men. Almost never in the collection does the speaker need to discover a truth he cannot then use. Always, when the speaker begins to speak, something has happened in his life which makes him need to know or to prove or to articulate some thing. This need is practical; and, if *knowing* implies intellectuality or an intellectual pursuit, the goal in most of the *Songs and Sonets* is not intellectual but moral: it answers the question *What do I do?*

Doing seems irrelevant to much of "The Extasie." The truth sought there seems to have nothing to do with *doing*. Yet it would be misleading to ignore the kinship of this poem with the rest of the *Songs and Sonets*. The intensity of the question in lines forty-nine and fifty brings the reader to bodies from the more rarefied atmosphere of the spirit and is a reminder that bodies have loomed large for all Donne's speakers and that none of them has been content with a world or with souls "whom no change can invade" (l. 48). Variety is, after all, love's sweetest part, a truth to which many of Donne's speakers would assent.

The force of almost every poem in the collection is toward the articulation of this moral concept: *this is right for us at this time*. This simple truth is the truth the casuists seek: it is occasional and limited, and it does not have to do with eschatology, for the broad outlines of the world are not in doubt for this man and this woman. If difficulties arise, they arise because of an epistemology which distinguishes between truth and its formulation. This man and this woman act in terms of structured reality, in terms of repeating patterns of behavior, even though that structured reality and those repeating patterns of behavior frequently do not show themselves. They act as if they mean to be harmonious with a harmonious world, and they merely ask *How can we be virtuous?*, seeking a truth which is severely limited in scope and which is "true" only for these two persons of the poem in their special circumstances.

As we see the relationship between "The Extasie" and others of the collection, we see that the argument of the last lines of the poem is not a falling off from the ecstasy described in the first forty-eight lines but the business of the poem. The problem facing these two persons is a simple one: *What are we to do?* The answer is equally simple: *act*. It is out of this simplicity the poems of the collection always come. But the problem has arisen because, the expression of truth conflicting, *what we are to do* is not clear. The question is simple, the answer is simple; the movement from the one to the other complicated and disturbing, and the astonishment felt at the conclusion of the poem lies not merely in the elegance of its cerebrations but in that Donne's speaker felt he had to bring that elegance to bear upon such a simple human need. "The Extasie" is not centrally concerned with metaphysics.

The answer to the question *What are we to do?*, "To'our bodies turne wee then," is an expansion of the simpler formulation, *act*. The lovers are to turn to bodies, the lovers' souls are to return to bodies, so that weak men may look upon revealed love. This observer, different in definition from that one posited in line twenty-one, is not of that select group of persons who "soules language understood" (l. 22). He is of that group to whom the speaker and his lover owe a certain patronizing responsibility, that man for whom love's mysteries remain mysteries until they are written down and explicated: "Loves mysteries in soules doe grow,/ But yet the body is his booke" (ll. 71-72). This weak man, like those who waited below the mountain for Moses, cannot look upon the face of truth and waits for it to be graven in stone.

More specifically, this weak man is one of those who, coming upon two lovers sitting silently and stilly upon a bank, sees only two silent and still persons. The love they express for each other, heretofore totally mental, is not visible to such weak men; and, as long as it remains totally mental, it will separate the lovers from mankind, which does not know that thcy lovc at all. As the speaker says "To'our bodies turne wee then," he suggests the action toward which he had argued through the poem, an action which expresses in visible terms the love which, in their ecstasy, they bear for one another. And, if the "you" of the poem responds favorably to the speaker, one can imagine the two lovers getting up from that bank, however pregnant, and moving off across the field or wood or garden, joining themselves more completely to the natural world and the world of sense and of men, and showing, by their visible pleasure and happiness, by their broad communion with their own and each other's bodies, their ecstasy.

Yet one senses that the "you" demurs before the end, perhaps expressing that the descent to bodies is, for her, a falling away from the earlier ecstasy. The speaker appears to respond to that hesitancy on her part when he refers again to that man who "soules language understood:"

> And if some lover, such as wee,
>   Have heard this dialogue of one,
> Let him still marke us, he shall see
>   Small change, when we'are to bodies gone. (ll. 73-76)

In short, getting up from this bank, the movement back into society, will result in small change for those like themselves, who will continue to understand the language of souls and consequently will continue to see the soul's ecstasy which they have achieved between them. It is this man's seeing *small change* which is the speaker's final trump card in his argument with the "you" of the poem. They can, he insists, retain this present ecstasy with small change, and, more wonderfully, can add immeasurably to it "when we'are to bodies gone." Going back to bodies, the lovers remain pure, and their ecstatic state remains, now enlarged and made human by revelation.

The electrifying effect of the closing passages of the poem is that nothing is excluded. The union of souls already achieved before the poem opens is maintained to and beyond the closing sounds of the speaker's voice, and what happens after that last word *gone* is not limited to that ecstasy of the souls and is, surely, inclusive, intimating the broadest range of expression of ecstatic love. We see these two lovers at the point when the two sepulchral statues begin to move again, but we know that as they begin to move again they reenter the world and subject themselves, to free themselves, to time and change. Beginning to move again on that bank, they reenter their lives, and everything becomes possible.[9]

The need for a new awareness which the speaker exhibits in the poem is made more trenchant by the speaker's clear knowledge of the consequences of error. This speaker, like others in the *Songs and Sonets,* knows that his immediate concern exists within the larger context of his "proper act and end." And, as he argues toward the particular action, he commits himself to a particular view of "what makes us man." If the speaker is wrong, therefore, he loses, at least, the ecstasy he had achieved before the poem began, and the return to bodies becomes in truth a falling away and a loss. In no other poem has the speaker wagered quite so much.

The admonition to action at the end of the poem, "To 'our bodies turne wee then," is a statement of satisfied and contented purpose, a statement which is the resolution of the conflict of the poem and which is the point toward which the speaker argued. The calm assurance of the line shows the speaker's knowledge that he has not denied the ecstasy they experienced together on the bank in favor of some inferior exercise. Nor has he made simple a complicated world. The simplicity of the action with which the poem closes is not of reduction but of expansion, for it reverberates with the complexity of the visible world. The admonition, weighed down and blurred by qualifications and made in the face of all that would prevent the speaker and his interlocutor from knowing and from being themselves, and arising out of the contradiction between inner and outer, the singular and the plural, is in itself expressive of the unity of the world, that sublime order which is the "government of things in God."

Donne's speaker's epistemology would resolve the apparent contradiction between the inner and the outer, the singular and the plural, and make whole, at least for two persons in their very special circumstances, the

world; for Donne's speaker believes in a relation be-
tween word and thing and between man's fact and
God's commandment which he is unable to prove. As he
does so, all things have become expressive of the truth
in God's mind. The conflicting multiplicity of the world
becomes, in itself, expressive of that sublime and calm
order which the speaker believes in but cannot see. He
says in "The Dreame," "Thou art so truth, that
thoughts of thee suffice,/To make dreames truths; and
fables histories" (ll. 7-8), and he knows, when he begins
to argue in any of the poems of the *Songs and Sonets,*
that dreams and truths and fables and histories may be
used interchangeably, being but words, and anything at
all, having an approximate and probable relation to
truth, may be counted as true and supportive of his
argument. Donne's speaker may then argue with some
rectitude toward a return to the bodies in "The Ex-
tasie," as he has in other places argued toward the
virtues of fornication or the occasional virtue of suicide
and as Hall and Escobar had argued for the sometime
virtue of murder, and he may support his plea with any
authority, as Escobar and Hall had done, without neces-
sarily believing in the probable truth of such authority.
As Taylor asserts in his wonderfully mixed metaphor:
"Whatsoever swims upon any water, belongs to this
exchequer."

Probability when one would prefer certainty; being
forced to choose among sins; these can never be appeal-
ing, and this might account for the unattractiveness of
casuistry in the present age. But casuistry, admitting
that law and truth conflict, that law and truth have no
immediate provable relationship, and that truth itself is
perceived as double, assumes a need for action and
provides a way of acting with the probability of recti-
tude if not the certainty of it.

Donne is never happy with the casuistry of probable opinions. In a letter of October 9, 1607, to Sir Thomas Lucy, he says: "The casuists are so indulgent, as that they allow a conscience to adhere to any probable opinion against a more probable, and do never bind him to seek out which is the more probable, but give him leave to dissemble it and to depart from it, if by mischance he come to know it" (Gosse, I, 174). This is *probabilism* which Donne disparages; at the same time, he accepts the traditional Anglican theory of *probabiliorism*. This latter theory does not work as well in practice because of the difficulty of finding the most probably right course of action. But, by accepting *probabiliorism,* Donne shows that he is willing to admit that the relation of law to truth is relative, not absolute. Despite his discomfiture, he makes a choice in the face of paradox.

He chooses inconstant love at one time, constant love another, secular love and spiritual love. In the middle of his life the casuistry of probable opinions may have allowed him to change his religion without loss of integrity and, later, to decide that all churches have, like all laws, some element of truth: "They are all virtual beams of one Sun, and wheresoever they find clay hearts, they harden them and moulder them into dust; and they entender and mollify waxen. They are not so contrary as the North and South Poles" (Gosse, I, 226). The compromise that Donne makes here is a compromise which all the casuists make in the face of a truth which is hard and inaccessible and whose formulation, as man sees it, is contradictory and paradoxical.

The relation of the truth to its formulation is at the heart of the problem of Donne's speaker's epistemology, and that is only another way of saying what Donne says in his letter of July 17, 1613: "A perpetual perplexity in the words cannot choose but cast a perplexity upon the things." Truth and the formulation of truth, thing and the word which stands for it, idea in the mind of God and the realization of that idea in a law: perplexity arises from these relationships, and compromise is the only human means of dealing with that perplexity. It is a compromise whose tension comes from enormous need for certainty and from broad acceptance of uncertainty. This unfulfilled need in the face of uncompromising reality and the compromise that arises from that hard dichotomy illustrate the near kinship of the speaker of these poems with the casuists of the seventeenth century. Their truths and the ways they found them were almost identical.

IV

The Speaker's Means to His End

Donne's speaker knows how lovers act:

> Let mee thinke any rivalls letter mine,
>   And at next nine
> Keepe midnights promise; mistake by the way
> The maid, and tell the Lady of that delay;
> Onely let mee love none, no, not the sport;
> From country grasse, to comfitures of Court,
> Or cities quelque choses, let report
>   My minde transport. ("Loves Usury," ll. 9-16)

Lovers experience all this hope, all this jealousy, this anticipation, confusion, and lovers may be filled with gaiety in the face of all this. A lover may be easily recognized. The sound of a man's voice may be recognizable, and the tone of that voice makes identification by name unnecessary: "Your worm is your only emperor for diet. We fat all creatures else to fat us, and we fat ourselves for maggots. Your fat king and your lean beggar is but variable service, two dishes, but to one table. That's the end." The way a person thinks can also be recognized, the way he puts his ideas together in his discourse, and the form of what he says. As the speaker of the *Songs and Sonets* argues again and again with his various listeners, defending his strange views against what he knows to be "moral," asserting that fornication is virtuous or that the separation of bodies is not all that it appears to be, arguing slyly at some times and solemnly at others, his voice and the way he speaks become familiar, as does the method of argument which he employs without regard to the kind of relationship between himself and his listener, to the issue at hand and without regard to the tone he takes with respect to that issue. This method serves the speaker when he chooses to see his situation in moral terms, and it is the method employed by the casuists of the seventeenth century and explained by them.

In speaking of the aim of the *Ductor Dubitantium,* Jeremy Taylor claims that, "although I have not given answers to every doubt, yet have I told what we are to do when any doubt arises; I have conducted the doubting conscience by such rules which in all doubts will declare her duty; and therefore if the matter of the doubt be in the reception of the sacrament of the eucharist, or in wearing clothes, or in eating, the rule is the same and applicable to every matter" (p. xx). Some of the rules have been suggested: one chooses a lesser sin over a greater; one serious authority establishes the probable truth of a course of action. There are others, and, taken together, they constitute a technique or device which in all cases leads to moral truth for the doubting conscience, regardless of the casuist or the particular issue. Because we have argument and because the argument is over a moral question, it is possible to formulate a kind of rhetoric of casuistry, a method which must be used in the discovery of moral truth. This rhetoric mounts to a poetic when we read the *Songs and Sonets*; the speaker employs the same means as the casuists, and the shape of his poems is entirely similar to the shape of cases of conscience.

The structure of the great majority of poems in the *Songs and Sonets* is familiar: suggested within the poem are two opposed positions relative to a moral issue. One of these usually is implicitly the position of the "you," and the other is explicitly the position of the speaker of the poem. The importance of this clear division is two-fold: it reinforces an understanding of the dramatic setting of the poem, and it makes explicit the knowledge that the poem is an argument between two established positions, not merely the articulation of the speaker's private views. The poems constitute cases for the defense, and the prosecution is present. It might have been possible for the speaker merely to assert his position; but without the clearly established counterposition, such a statement would remain merely statement, capable of rebuttal outside the poem.

As the speaker argues in defense of his private perception of truth, he appeals, like the casuists, to the authority of law. Escobar, in this respect, is typical of all the casuists: "Is it permissible for innocent persons to be reduced to slavery in a just war? [A] Palao says so, because they are members of a guilty state, which has dominion over their liberty and may dispose of it, just as they themselves and their parents could in necessity" (pp. 125-26). We see here in this case the casuist opposing one law, which is in reality Palao's *opinion* about the law, to a law which is more probably true: *it is impermissible to reduce innocent persons to slavery.* This appeal to the authority of law and the casuist's clear juxtaposition of two conflicting laws suggest an important fact about the poems of the *Songs and Sonets*. The major conflict of the poems, like the cases, is stated in terms of a conflict among laws. The major structural element of the poems is formulations of or opinions about law, and the argument of the poems progresses from stage to stage as laws are introduced, not, as in some other poems, as emotions or sensory perceptions are introduced.

In another kind of poem the major structural element is the visual image. In Herrick's poem, "Upon Julia's Clothes," the forward progress of that poem is measured in terms of visual or sensory impressions accumulating to a whole. "Silks" in which Julia goes dissolves into "liquefaction of her clothes," and "That brave Vibration" resounds in "glittering." Each of the images is descriptive and, in a way, analytic and together they mount to a re-creation of the impression Julia makes upon the speaker. The opening passages of "The Love Song of J. Alfred Prufrock" are equally descriptive, but the major structural element is the progressive stages of the narrative as the "you and I" move through "half-deserted streets."

But notice "The broken heart." The poem argues toward a moral question, and the progressive stages of the argument are formed by a reference to law. In the situation of the poem, the speaker, speaking to a female "you," recognizes that he has fallen in love, and what is heard in the words of the poem constitutes an analysis of that action. The central action of the poem is contained in lines nineteen and twenty: "I brought a heart into the roome,/But from the roome, I carried none with mee," and progressively through the poem this action is referred to one law after another in a double attempt to discover the moral nature of the action and the consequence of it. This seems to be characteristic of Donne.

The resort to law begins in the first lines of the poem: "He is starke mad, who ever sayes,/That he hath been in love an houre" (ll. 1-2), where the speaker is asserting his peculiar understanding of the law of love. The next two lines elaborate, and the next four present the same law in different images:

> Who will beleeve mee, if I sweare
> That I have had the plague a year?
> Who would not laugh at mee, if I should say,
> I saw a flaske of *powder burne a day?* (ll. 5-8)

Love, the plague, and the powder all three are asserted to have immediate effect; and, insofar as law defines characteristic behavior, the three images of the stanza are laws governing the characteristic behavior of three things: love, plague, and powder. The second stanza in like manner asserts the law that love is all-consuming:

> All other griefes allow a part
>   To other griefes, and aske themselves but some;
> They come to us, but us Love draws,
> Hee swallows us, and never chawes: (ll. 11-14)

And the last two lines of the stanza assert that the law of love is like the law of chained shot and the pike:

> By him, as by chain'd shot, whole rankes doe dye,
> He is the tyran Pike, our hearts the Frye. (ll. 15-16)

Love operates in these ways, and the consequence of bringing a heart into a room and carrying none out again is to have it broken. The speaker moves his argument forward by reference to images which suggest laws of behavior, and those laws enable him to assert confidently that what has happened to his heart is that "Love, alas,/At one first blow did shiver it as glasse" (ll. 23-24). Yet that is not enough, for the speaker knows other laws:

> Yet nothing can to nothing fall,
>   Nor any place be empty quite,

> Therefore I thinke my breast hath all
> Those peeces still, though they be not unite. (ll. 25-28)

And like the law which governs the behavior of broken mirrors, "My ragges of heart can like, wish, and adore,/ But after one such love, can love no more" (ll. 31-32). The shivered heart is the consequence of action, falling in love. It is the punishment for one grand sin. There are poems, like Donne's own "Holy Sonnet XVIII," which appear to be arguments toward an action; yet this poem is significantly different from most of the poems in the *Songs and Sonets*. The admonition to action in this poem, "Betray kind husband thy spouse to our sights" (l. 11), is not the focus of the poem. The poem requests definition:

> Betray kind husband thy spouse to our sights,
> And let myne amorous soule court thy mild Dove,
> Who is most trew, and pleasing to thee, then
> When she'is embrac'd and open to most men. (ll. 11-14)

The sonnet is an argument toward a definition of the spouse of Christ, and the progressive stages of the argument are formed by successive statements and questions:

> What! is it She, which on the other shore
> Goes richly painted? or which rob'd and tore
> Laments and mournes in Germany and here?
> Sleepes she a thousand, then peepes up one yeare?
> Is she selfe truth and errs? now new, now outwore? (ll. 2-6)

Each question and statement suggests the concluding statement, and the poem moves forward by those progressive steps toward definition. This holy sonnet is unusual in that respect; "The broken heart" is far more characteristic.

Donne's verse normally employs law to progress.

The poems, arising out of conflict between the speaker and the "you," concern themselves with moral issues; and, as they do, they move from one statement of characteristic behavior to another statement of characteristic behavior. These statement need not, of course, necessarily be statements of the characteristic behavior of *humans*. The characteristic behavior of plagues and mirrors does as well, for all law is expressive of the truth in God's mind. The line "Like gold to ayery thinnesse beate," though justifiably famous, is characteristic.

A distinction is made here between the image and the metaphor, of which the image is a part. The metaphor is expressive of other things and will be discussed later. The image which makes the metaphor is, however, expressive of laws of characteristic behavior, and the images of almost any poem make the point. "The Funerall" and "The Relique" are two poems concerned with the same or a similar situation, and the central image of each is the same: "A bracelet of bright haire about the bone" ("The Relique," l. 6). In each poem, it is the bracelet of hair *as it operates* with which the poet is concerned. It is the function of the bracelet that is at issue, and the nature of the bracelet—what the moral theologians would call "its proper act and end"—enters into the poem only as that "proper act and end" leads to action, that is, as it is expressive of law. In the first stanza of "The Relique," the bracelet is said to be possibly "some way/To make their soules, at the last busie day,/Meet at this grave, and make a little stay" (ll. 9-11). Even the paper on which the poem is written is not handled in itself but only in its function: "I would have that age by this paper taught/What miracles wee harmelesse lovers wrought" (ll. 21-22). In "The Funerall," the bracelet's importance in the poem is the same: it is important as it functions. The soul "Will leave this [bracelet] to controule,/And keepe these limbes, her Provinces, from dissolution" (ll. 7-8). The second stanza of "The Funerall" presents three images, of the nerves, of the hairs in the bracelet, and of the manacles of prisoners, each of which is described in what it does rather than in what it is or in what it looks like. Bracelets shackle bone together, people together, body and soul together, and the speaker of these poems is interested in that fact about bracelets and not in other things that might have been said. We see these bracelets as they exist in time and in space, and what we know of their appearance, their weight and feel leads us on to the more important understanding: their place in the patterned and reticulated world. These bracelets do things, and as they act we find them articulating the law of their own behavior.

This resort to law, necessary to moral argument, and the employment of the image to express law, gives the speaker of these poems access to understandings which would otherwise be closed to him. Beyond the concept of the tripartite law, defined by Aquinas and employed by all the casuists of the seventeenth century, is a more general and more submerged understanding: the world repeats itself and patterns form, and one may generalize upon experience. As images are expressive of law, of what is *generally* true, they express for the speaker a vital concept: there is order, and order in the world may be expressed. Beyond this, there is further knowledge. The image is not merely expressive of the speaker's belief that the world is ordered, but, more profoundly, is itself proof of that order. And, as the image is apprehended, the world comes within the speaker's grasp. The images of these poems are devices whereby the speaker may break through and go beyond ratiocination about patterns and seize the thing itself.

The speaker, knowing this, describes things as they exist in time and as they express the law of their being. Surely the most famous image in the *Songs and Sonets* is the one presented in the last twelve lines of "A Valediction: forbidding mourning":

> If they be two, they are two so
>   As stiffe twin compasses are two,
> Thy soule, the fixt foot, makes no show
>   To move, but doth, if the'other doe.
>
> And though it in the center sit,
>   Yet when the other far doth rome,
> It leanes, and hearkens after it,
>   And growes erect, as that comes home.
>
> Such wilt thou be to mee, who must
>   Like th'other foot, obliquely runne;
> Thy firmnes makes my circle just,
>   And makes me end, where I begunne. (ll. 25-36)

One confronts here a thing essentially simple: the image of a tool being used properly for that end to which it was designed and as the function of the tool is apprehended, the simple opening and closing and the movement of the legs as the circle is traced, there is nothing about compasses beyond what one knows that one needs to know. The speaker has given his listener and the reader access to ultimate truth. Expressed as law—that is, expressed as a statement of how the compass behaves—the image, deceptively simple, reverberates with that which is clear, precise, scientific, and final. The description of it is a description of the thing itself, and it rings with the clarity of final pronouncements.

As the images are expressive of law, they are expressive of universal truth. What is known of this compass is what is known of all compasses. *Difference* here is unknown; the image is expressive of what joins and not what separates. This seems to be true of the great majority of Donne's images in the *Songs and Sonets*. As localized as they are and as precisely defined, they suggest the species, not the individual. Their tendency is to be seen as type. In "The Relique," the "bracelet of bright haire about the bone" is possibly seen by different persons in the first two stanzas. The first person is said to "thinke that there a loving couple lies" (l. 8), with the suggestion that whoever "digs" the bracelet has seen others like it and has known men who wore them and the reasons for that wearing. In the second stanza there is the suggestion that

> If this fall in a time, or land,
> Where mis-devotion doth command,
> Then, he that digges us up, will bring
> Us, to the Bishop, and the King.
> To make us Reliques. (ll. 12-16)

The speaker sees himself as one of a class, either of lovers or of fake saints, and his image then is of that which is general. Being so, the speaker's images have all the vitality and all the beauty and all the power of mass and concerted movement. They describe one thing as it moves like other things, and they gain power from their reflection of many things moving as one. There are built into the fabric of the verse living ideas, ideas expressive intrinsically of movement, of people and plants and animals and things living and operating in their patterned way in the space of the world.

There is no suggestion here that Donne's images are like Ben Jonson's, whose images are frequently said to suggest the class or type and not the specific thing. The following passage from Jonson's "To Penshurst" illustrates the difference:

Thou hast thy walkes for health, as well as sport:
Thy *Mount,* to which the *Dryads* doe resort,
Where Pan, and Bacchus their high feasts have made,
Beneath the broad beech, and the chest-nut shade;
That taller tree, which of a nut was set,
At his great birth, where all the *Muses* met.
There, in the writhed barke, are cut the names
Of many a Sylvane, taken with his flames.
And thence, the ruddy *Satyres* oft provoke
The lighter *Faunes,* to reach thy *Ladies oke.* (ll. 9-18)

The visual image of the prospect at Penshurst is painted, and the consequence is a landscape, presented for us as it appears to the viewer, not as it is in itself. Each element of the description is dependent upon Jonson's powers of observation. There is no coherence in this description; the beeches and chestnuts could as well be maples and red oaks. There is no *conclusion,* except the conclusion that Jonson gives the reader. Penshurst is idealized, and, as it is so, is like no other house that man ever saw. By contrast, Donne's speaker's images, as they attempt to define the way things do behave, mount easily from the particular to the general and take the reader along with them to truths which would be inaccessible otherwise.

As Donne's speaker's images move from "bright haire about the bone," from the extreme particularity inherent in the three aspects of the image, "bright," "haire," "bone," to the manner in which the bracelet is like all bracelets, inductive reasoning may be seen, the movement from particular to universal truth. One may say that the "truth" is what Aquinas calls "the government of things in God," that as one defines a compass or a flower or the sun rising or a bracelet or a flea, one is describing in a not entirely negligible way an idea in the mind of God. But one need not take a seventeenth-century view. Even for the seventeenth century, law is defined as a statement of characteristic behavior; as one can see the behavior of this individual replicating the behavior of another and another, one is assured that, God or no, the world is partially amenable to one's sense. And that if it is not *totally* amenable, what one knows of it in the compass or the bracelet or the flea is a symbol for what one does not know of it. The image presents for the speaker's listener a limited but final truth, and it is luminous with a final and unlimited truth.

This resort to law, of which the image is an expression, is an appeal from what Ames called "mans fact" to the authority of "Gods Commandement," from one perception of truth to another separate expression of truth. This appeal is an attempt to make reasonable and public a truth which is private and intuitive. It is an appeal from the emotion to the intellect: one feels an action to be correct, one wishes to understand that it is correct. It is an attempt to articulate faith. And it is finally an attempt to prove that there is no disjunction between various perceptions of truth, between emotion and intellect, feeling and understanding. While there are significant differences between the Puritans, the Anglicans, and the Jesuits on many issues, one of the most important being the relative reliance of each of them on reason or faith, Anglican, Puritan, and Jesuit alike felt that faith must be articulated. Perry Miller, in his extraordinary study of Puritanism in New England, places a correct and important emphasis on the reasonableness of that articulation; and what he says of the Puritans, the most extremely pietistic of all of them, is true as well of the rest: "No matter how irrational the government of God may seem to His uncomprehending creatures, it is so only in appearance. Faith is called upon to believe, not merely in redemption, but in the reason behind all things. The regenerated intellect may not understand 'abstract wisdom,' but it can catch at least a glimmering. By the very fact of being regenerated the intellect is duty-bound to strive for such a glimpse" (p. 69). As Donne's speaker is heard arguing with the "you" of the *Songs and Sonets,* associating what is private and intuitive and mysterious with the "reason behind all things," the nature of this appeal to law is more clearly understood. The speaker's intuition of himself, like the casuist's private perception of truth, is nowhere provable in experience. It is a *direct* apprehension of truth, and it cannot be dealt with intellectually in itself. Its formulation must be altered so as to make it amenable to the reason. Walter J. Ong, writing on medieval lyrics, makes an important point: "Although truth is founded on the real, is in touch with the real, we can get into intellectual contact with reality only by the peculiar operation known as abstraction" (p. 325). Law is an abstraction; and, as the casuist and the speaker of these poems need to understand intellectually their emotional response to a particular situation, as they sense the need to understand their private perception of truth, they "abstract" that private truth in terms of the law.

This is, in fact, the creation of metaphor. The law, "Gods commandement," has never been fully expressive of "mans fact" and one can only act in a particular case as if the law were fully applicable. Or, stated another way, one can only act in the particular case like those whose situation is perfectly covered by the law. While using, therefore, the instrument of reason, rational discourse, to solve their cases of conscience, the casuists engage in the central business of poetry. Returning to the moral truth asserted by Escobar, referred to in the last chapter: "The man who has been justly condemned may not flee from prison" (p. 113), one finds that this formulation of truth unites a law and a statement of fact about a particular man, and it seems to imply no disjunction between them. Yet the statement about the man, that he has been justly condemned, is not sufficiently expressive of his state. There may be extenuating circumstances which qualify the justness of his condemnation, and after that condemnation, there may be peculiarities in his situation which suggest that to keep him in prison would be cruel and unusual punishment. The general law is still true. But the doubting conscience's intuition of itself, derived from a different source, makes that general law only partially applicable, and as the doubting conscience chooses to follow the law and to remain in prison, he chooses to ignore all the ways that the law is inapplicable and to act *as if* it were perfectly applicable. Father Ong says, "For both poetry and theology, metaphor is a last, and not quite satisfactory, resort" (p. 337).

The truth about themselves which the speaker attempts to articulate and understand is a truth incapable of rational expression and does not derive from ratiocinative processes. Invariably, when that truth is expressed in these poems, it is expressed as a logical paradox, a statement in which the subject contradicts the predicate: "Our two soules therefore, which are one" ("A Valediction: forbidding mourning," l. 21). As the speaker attempts to understand that truth and to place it within the larger world outside himself, he asserts that it is like those truths which are, in fact, understandable:

> Our two soules therefore, which are one,
>   Though I must goe, endure not yet
> A breach, but an expansion,
>   Like gold to ayery thinnesse beate. (ll. 21-24)

The reader understands the law of gold's behavior: if pure enough, it is malleable enough to be beaten thin enough—endlessly—without the separation of molecule from molecule, until its heavy weight is dissipated by its extension. As the speaker asserts this law of the behavior of gold and as he asserts that he and she are exactly like gold, we sense the truth of them which they are not able to prove inductively of themselves: *they are one.* The speaker has asserted that the law of gold's behavior is exactly expressive of himself and his interlocutor in the same way the casuists assert that one or another law is exactly expressive of a particular situation—when both the speaker and the casuist know that *no* formulation of law is exactly expressive of *any* particular situation.

When the speaker asserts *this law fully applies,* giving reasonable expression to unreasonable truth, we see the source of the tension in Donne's poetry. The violent coupling of heterogeneous *things* of which Samuel Johnson spoke is not the central locus of the excitement nor the disturbing quality of Donne's poetry in the *Songs and Sonets.* The excitement of Donne's poetry is in the contradiction between idea and articulation. An unreasonable truth has been subjected to rational analysis; "mans fact" has been subjected to "Gods Commandement," and the disjunction between the one and the many ignored. And Donne's speaker, as he gives full rational analysis to his images, acts as if he is giving full rational analysis to the speaker's paradoxical truth. Reason must abstract, of course, and reason abstracts as it confronts this poetry: the image is concentrated on in reasoning these things out, and, like the casuists, one depends upon faith that the reasoned explanation actually explains what is not reasonable.

Consequently, what was thought in the metaphor to

be a contrast between two unlike things joined together, is seen now to be a contradiction between reason and those things with which the reason must deal. What is perceived in the metaphor is absolutely separate from and contradictory of what one had been led to expect in the image. Violence has been done to reason, and one knows that rational argument has forced irrational conclusions.

One is not, in the end, astonished by any of Donne's comparisons, by the speaker saying that one thing is *like* another, no matter how strange the comparison; for nothing, one supposes, astonishes once it becomes familiar, and everything loses its edge as one becomes easy and comfortable with the similarity among things. The response may of course be illuminated—after many readings—by the first reading. One may remember the *first* astonishment at Donne's speaker's yoking disparate things together and the hard beauty of those images: "bright haire" and "gold to ayery thinnesse beate." But the astonishment becomes, after a time, an astonishment only remembered. What one is never comfortable with—because one can never be familiar with it and can never assimilate it—is what one is forced to do with reason: express in reasoned language that which is neither reasonable nor capable of expression. The reader and the speaker of these poems know that the kinds of things that may be said about gold are different kinds of things from what may be said about lovers who pretend to unity. The two kinds of truth are discrete, the one rational, the other something else, but certainly not rational; and the kind of investigation to which gold may be subjected is different in kind from the investigation to which lovers may be subjected. *This* being like *that,* whatever the terms of the comparison, may finally cease to interest, but other kinds of assertions may retain their liveliness.

The reasoned articulation of unreasonable truths is similar to medical attempts to explain the function of memory through chemical formulas. The attempt to explain through chemistry how it is that one is still chilled by the memory of "Bath'd in cold quicksilver sweat" ("The Apparition," l. 12) violates one's sense of self and of poetry; and yet, the knowledge that one is in fact defined as a mere sequence of chemical reactions makes one surrender to the attempt, knowing it to be necessary. All the while, what one can say about oneself as a chemical reaction has nothing to do with what one may say about oneself as chilled by jealousy.

Donne's speaker's method is constantly to subject paradoxes to rational expression and analysis; his method constantly astonishes. One can never become accustomed to one's reason being violated in this manner. The speaker's method of articulation is continuously alive, constantly mercurial, and, like the speaker's own private truth, incapable of explication. Consequently, a minimal definition of the metaphor as it is employed by Donne's speaker in the *Songs and Sonets* might run something like the following: it is not simply or even mainly characterized by strangeness of comparison. It is characterized by the speaker's—and the reader's—sense of contradiction between two truths, one interior and one exterior, the interior truth being tentative and derived from sources other than the rational, the exterior truth having the force of authority and being capable of rational analysis. The metaphor presents the interior truth as if it had reached its fullest expression in the exterior.[1]

The speaker's attempt, in the casuistry of the *Songs*

and Sonets, to articulate and support a privately per-
ceived truth and to do so in terms of law, requires a
logical method, a device for ordering the argument of
the poem in such a way as to arrive at the truth he
needs. It is necessary to address the problem of the
particular method of argument employed by these
casuists, all of whom were concerned with the *workings*
of the faculty of conscience, with its component parts
and the relationship among them. H. R. McAdoo, writ-
ing on seventeenth-century moral theology, says that
"Conscience has two parts, *synteresis,* or the power by
which we hold and understand general principles of
morality, and *conscientia,* by which we apply these
principles to specific actions in order to assess their
rightness and wrongness. Conscience is a function of the
practical intellect. It is the mind of man passing moral
judgments" (p. 66). *Conscientia* is the method by which
these casuists apply the law to the particular situation,
and as they face *conscientia,* they face the problem of
the kind of logic employed in the cases of conscience.[2]

Of the two important forms of logic prevalent in the
seventeenth century, Ramist and Aristotelian, we find
that most of the Protestants were Ramist, including
William Ames, Richard Hooker, William Perkins, and
Joseph Hall. The Jesuits on the other hand are clearly
Peripatetic. As one studies the cases and compares the
Protestant and Jesuit works one discovers that they are
argued in almost exactly the same way, and the contro-
versy of the sixteenth and seventeenth centuries over
the two modes of logic disappears in the cases them-
selves. It is necessary to distinguish between, on the one
hand, treatises like Azor's and Jeremy Taylor's, each of
which employs one or the other kind of logic in its
analysis of the workings of conscience, and, on the
other, the specific cases of conscience contained in

those works. An analysis of *conscience* may proceed in any of a variety of ways; a question of morality may be argued in only one way.

The central device of logic to which the casuists resorted, at least so they thought, was the syllogism:

> *He that lives in sinne, shall dye:*
> *I live in sinne:*
> Therefore, *I shall dye.* (p. 3)

William Ames, who gives us this syllogism, says of it that "in that syllogisme alone is contained the whole nature of conscience. The proposition treateth of the Law; the Assumption of the fact or state, and the Conclusion of the relation arising from the fact or state, in regard of that Law; the Conclusion either pronounceth one guilty, or giveth spiritual peace and security" (p. 4).

The syllogism is of course central to Peripatetic logic, and it has a place in the logic of the Ramists, though of reduced importance. Describing Ramus's "fundamental philosophy," Miller says,

Before Adam lost the image of God, Ramus said, almost all of his judgments had been simply axiomatical; in his integrity he had been able to see and to pronounce sentence immediately, as when he named the animals; he had uttered what was true and perceived what was false, and had discoursed by infallible progression from one proposition to its inevitable successor. Ideally all good judgments—sermons, reflections, poems—ought to be such a series of self-evident axioms, arranged in artistic sequence. But fallen man generally comes to conclusions through love, hate, envy, or cupidity rather than through perception. Therefore today men must use the syllogism in order by its constancy to animate their judgments, "otherwise all our assertions will be levity, error, temerity, not judgment." (p. 133)

The logician should "use the syllogism only when in doubt about formulating a particular proposition, or when incapable of recognizing the order of precedence among several statements" (p. 134). It is clear that the syllogism is central even to Ramistic logic insofar as the logician is unclear or in doubt about "formulating a particular proposition." In moral questions, the casuist may not argue simply from self-evident axioms because, by definition in the case of conscience, there are no self-evident axioms; he must resort to syllogism. We appear here to be faced with a position in which, whether the casuist is Peripatetic or Ramistic in his persuasion, he will be employing the syllogism in his argument.

As the Ramist does so, he appears to use most prominently two forms of the composite syllogism, the "hypothetical" and the "disjunctive." Miller distinguishes between them this way: "The hypothetical meant reasoning thus: 'If there are Gods, there is divination'; the disjunctive meant this construction: 'It is either day or night, it is not day, therefore it is night' " (p. 136). As the logician is in doubt, whether he is Ramistic or Peripatetic, he resorts to one form or another of the syllogism.

But we see that the process of reasoning in the cases of conscience is not syllogistic—whether the syllogism be Ramistic or Peripatetic. The cases begin with a major premise, as Ames says: *He that lives in sinne, shall dye.* That premise is accepted as perfectly true, but, despite Ames, the minor premise may run: *I am virtuous.* The major premise and the minor premise of the syllogism of casuistry have nothing to do with each other. They are discrete. Donne's own *Biathanatos* is illustrative. The book begins each of its several parts with the assumption that, according to various kinds of law, suicide is sinful: yet the subtitle of the book and the major effort of all the argument in the book is to prove that it "is not so Naturally Sinne, that it may never be otherwise."

All the casuists, and their discussions of murder are illustrative, begin with the assumption that there is a law denying the validity of the action they propose to justify; and they assert that that major premise is not applicable to their cases. It is as if someone had said, *All men are mortals,* and his interlocutor responded, *That is perfectly true; but I am a plant.* This process of reasoning is not syllogistic but rather, in a backward fashion, a process in which the minor premise is posed first and major premises searched for which will be apposite. Donne says on the title page of *Biathanatos* that in it "The Nature, and the extent of all those Lawes, which seeme to be violated by this Act [suicide], are diligently surveyed," expressing for us the movement of his thought. A law of behavior has been given which has great probability of truth and which seems to be universally accepted. The casuist argues against that law by denying its applicability to the present case. He does not deny its truth. As he argues, he poses first one and then another and then another law or opinion about law, which, as true as the initially posed law, have a greater applicability. And the process of reasoning exhibited here distinguishes among the applicability of various laws. The casuist forcefully asserts the special nature of his case.

The shape of the argument of the great majority of poems in the *Songs and Sonets* is not syllogistic. The speaker of the poems faces a premise suggested by the "you" of the poem and his response to that premise is to say, *That does not apply.* The position of the "you" and that of the speaker are discrete. Compare, by contrast, the syllogistic arrangement of "To His Coy Mistress," by Andrew Marvell. The first several lines of each of the verse paragraphs, taken together, form a syllogism:

Major premise: Had we but World enough, and Time,
                 This coyness Lady were no crime. (ll. 1—2)

Minor premise: But at my back I alwaies hear
                 Times winged Charriot hurrying near. (ll. 21-22)

Conclusion: Now therefore, while the youthful hew
                 Sits on thy skin like morning glew,
                 And while thy willing Soul transpires
                 At every pore with instant Fires,
                 Now let us sport us while we may. (ll. 33—37)

The movement from the major to the minor is smooth and easy, and, at each stage of the argument, the speaker brings his interlocutor along with him. The complexities of tone in the concluding paragraph, the possibility that the speaker is more than slightly ironic in the point to which he argues, does not vitiate the fact that the structure of his argument, if not the total effect of that argument, is syllogistic. The speaker moves from a clearly stated major premise to a clearly stated minor premise, to a conclusion; and the syllogism itself is expressive of the total argument. By employing the disjunctive syllogism, the speaker of the poem includes within the syllogism the position of the "you" of the poem. The coyness of the lady is shown to be a crime because of the axiomatic truth which presupposes there is not "World enough, and Time." There is, in the *Songs and Sonets,* no such clear relation between the position of the "you" and the minor premise of the syllogism. In the syllogistic arrangement of Marvell's poem, the speaker places himself and his interlocutor within the syllogism and in the course of the poem proves his interlocutor wrong. On the other hand, the speaker of the *Songs and Sonets,* assenting to probabilism, has no such need or desire. The "you" of the poems may not *be* wrong, and one does not know in any case. What one can know, and what the speaker asserts, is that the "you" of the poems is positing a merely inapplicable truth.

We need then to look again at the shape of the cases of conscience and at the manner in which they employ reason to deal with moral questions. Clearly, they do not employ the syllogism, either Ramistic or Peripatetic; and, as clearly, their shape and structure are peculiar to themselves. Virtually always, a case of conscience begins with a question, the formulation of which implies the answer: *yes*. Escobar asks a typical question: "Is it permissible for a member of a religious order to kill a slanderer who is asserting that he has committed serious violations of his religious vows?" (p. 119). The implicit answer *yes* is the point to be argued toward, and whether Ramistic or Peripatetic, the elements of the argument will be laws or opinions about laws, each of which is supportive of that *yes*. The answer Escobar gives to this question is the following:

Father Amicus, . . . *On Justice* Vol. 5 ch. 36 sec. 7 #118, is not so bold as to give an affirmative reply, lest he seem to be opposed to the general opinion. However, he writes as follows, for the sake of argument. "If this is permissible for a layman," he says, "for the sake of his honor and reputation, it seems that it is much more permissible for a clergyman and a member of a religious order; just as profession, wisdom, and virtue from which honor arises for the clergy and the religious in this life are greater than dexterity in weapons from which honor arises for the laity. Again, it is permissible to the clergy and the religious to kill a thief in defense of their own 'possessions,' if no other method is available: therefore they may also do so in defense of their honor." (p. 119)

After hedging at the beginning of his answer, Escobar warms to his subject toward the end and concludes, "It is permissible."[3]

As the casuist argues backward from the minor to the major premise of the syllogism, as he attempts to prove that "it is permissible," he appears to argue inductively, from particular facts to general principles. He appears in the argument to suggest that, as he acts in this particular way and as it is true that many men act this way, it is certainly true that all men act in this way. But inductive reasoning enters into the cases of conscience only in a tangential manner. The probable truth of a law may be established inductively, as suggested in the discussion of the compass image in "A Valediction: forbidding mourning," but once a law is established as probable, neither the casuist nor the poet argues inductively. The truth of a general principle in the case of conscience does not rest upon its antecedent in the particular case. The law is received from exterior sources, not derived from particular cases, and there is no way to establish the validity of a general principle from the facts at hand. In an interesting question, Escobar asks,

Say that some horseman is fleeing from a pursuing enemy, and he sees a child or a beggar lying on the road; he must either run them down or be struck with a mortal blow by his enemy; which should he choose? [A] He is obliged to use whatever circumspection is possible, so as not to cause harm; but he is not obliged to stand his ground and perish at the hands of his enemy; because he has the right to flee by going along a public road, of which right he cannot be deprived by reason of somebody lying someplace accidentally. Lessius, Bk. 2 Ch. 9 quest. 59 #3. Someone has appropriately added, "unless the child that would be killed is unbaptized"; for then the fleeing rider would be obliged by the law of charity to die rather than to kill him. (p. 120-21)

Leaving one's astonishment at this case, it is clear that the validity of the general principle governing unbaptized babies is established through the theory of *probabilism,* and induction does not enter the argument. Further, there is no inductive progression from Escobar's nightrider to the general principle governing unbaptized babies; nightriders and babies are discrete in logic and on the highroad, and nothing connects them in either arena, except that the law governing unbaptized babies limits the law governing the use of the highways. The resort to law in the case has the paradoxical effect of particularizing the situation. Unbaptized babies and the laws governing their murder in the highroads, being present, make special the nightrider's situation. In short, the process of reasoning in the cases is neither inductive nor deductive; it is something else for which there is no name: the universal principle operates in these cases to *individualize*. This process of reasoning is precisely the process we find in the metaphors of the poems of the *Songs and Sonets*.

As the images become metaphors, as they are similar in some way to the speaker's conception of his situation, they are employed to particularize the speaker's situation. They are chosen and juxtaposed in such a way as to increase one's sense of the special nature of his case. The poems are occasional in nature, and, in that, they are like cases of conscience. They come out of particular situations, and they attempt to answer particular needs. The speaker may then prove that the position of the "you" is inapplicable only if he may forcefully assert that his circumstances differ from those of most men. The poems of the *Songs and Sonets* assert such a difference. The speaker knows that he may not maintain his own position in the face of the general law unless he may prove that the general law must be altered by circumstance. The speaker never argues against the truth of the position of the "you." He argues against its being perfectly applicable in the present case. The particularity of the poems, for which they are famous, the presentation of a lively and local reality may be a consequence of the kind of mind and genius which the poet possessed. And surely Donne's ability to give to "airy nothing/A local habitation and a name"—in Theseus's phrase—is a consequence of his ability and not his choice of form. Yet within the context of each poem, the localness operates with respect to other elements of the poem in certain ways. And it may be expressive not only of Donne's genius but of Donne's kind of genius, which seems to be moral as well as poetic.

Donne seems most to be engaged by those things which separate man from man and from his context. The flea, having bitten the two people in that poem, separates them from all those not bitten, and the limiting nature of the concluding images of "The Canonization" separates them from the generality. Even when the speaker finds the two of them in accord with a universal pattern, the pattern itself is strange. It can be accepted, for example, that it is a "truth" that virtuous men do pass mildly away, and, in the ease and confidence of their going, they go from one plane of existence to another soundlessly. Yet because of common experience the parting of lovers is known to be a separation of bodies and consequently may be a cause for distress, and that knowledge is not vitiated by the speaker's asserting that the separation of bodies is like the quiet going forth of a satisfied and serene soul. Even when the lovers are asserted to be like other men, the other men they are asserted to be like are so exotic as to make the comparison tend to increase rather than decrease one's sense of their specialness.

In poem after poem after poem, the speaker asserts as the decisive law governing his situation a law which directly contradicts the law that had apparently governed the position of the "you" of the poem. In "The Sunne Rising," the "you" of the poem, the sun itself, appears to have asserted the pervasive effect of time;

for, as it has moved about the earth, it has governed the life cycles of schoolboys, poor apprentices, court huntsmen, country ants, and now appears to assert that "to thy motions lovers seasons run" (l. 4). Arguing against that notion, the speaker, in the second stanza and then finally in the third, asserts that time, as it is evidenced in the motions of the sun, has nothing to do with the lovers, for they are between them both night and day:

> Looke, and to morrow late, tell mee,
> Whether both the'India's of spice and Myne
> Be where thou leftst them, or lie here with mee. (ll. 16-18)

It was the *motion* of the sun which, the sun asserted, called forth the lovers from their beds. It is now the contraction of the earth into their bed, the fact that they are all the world which, as an image, not merely contradicts the sun's contention but *nullifies* it, that the speaker poses. Insofar as they are all the world, the sun is "everywhere" (l. 29), and his motions cease absolutely. Posing the image of them as all the world, as a law, denies the validity of the sun's argument. As an image, in itself, it does not astonish. But as a law governing behavior and when applied to the two lovers in their situation, it denies the validity of a law which certainly has greater probability: that lovers do, after all, "run" to the sun's motions.

The validity of the sequences of images in the third stanza of "The Canonization" is equally expressive. The essential *ordinariness* of lovers is the point argued against, and the sequence of images in the stanza is to the position of the "you" what the opinions of "serious authorities" are to the law. "Call her one, mee another flye" (l. 20), we hear; the suggestion of insignificance in "flye" barely covers the submerged suggestions of mortality and furious, destructive sex, both of which lead the speaker in the next line to "We'are Tapers too, and at our owne cost die" (l. 21). This process, where each image builds on the preceding one, is used to define and restrict the applicability of the speaker's truth. Only insofar as they are flies and tapers can they be seen as "the'Eagle and the Dove" (l. 22). Insignificance here in the fly has burgeoned into the imperious eagle and the quiet dove, and both, "being one," become the phoenix: "So to one neutrall thing both sexes fit" (l. 25), an image which sums up the images of sex-in-flight, self-destruction, division-collapsing-to-addition and adds to them the special fact of resurrection: "Wee dye and rise the same, and prove/Mysterious by this love" (ll. 26-27). Through this series of images, the speaker has asserted the validity of his own view of his love, but, by appealing to the images of the stanza, the speaker has carefully restricted the applicability of his assertion.

In this particular case, he says, despite what may be generally true, this particular thing is true. And one understands in consequence the importance of the last stanza and the conclusion of the argument: "And thus invoke us; You whom reverend love/Made one anothers hermitage" (ll. 37-38). *Love* is not asserted here to be this important; the speaker refrains from making the general statement. Love is asserted to be important only in the special circumstances of the third stanza as recapitulated and refined in the last. Answering the "you" at the end, the speaker pleads for the importance of his love *only* for those

> . . . to whom love was peace, that now is rage;
>   Who did the whole worlds soule contract, and drove
>   Into the glasses of your eyes
>   (So made such mirrors, and such spies,
>   That they did all to you epitomize,)
> Countries, Townes, Courts. (ll. 39-44)

The applicability of the command is severely qualified. Casuistry, concerned with particular cases, is concerned with particular application of law. The more particular the case, the more likely it is that the casuist will arrive at a judgment opposed to general acceptance. Donne's paradoxical conclusion here would not seem strange in a book of casuistry. By determining that his speaker is henceforth a "patterne" (l. 45), he becomes as much an authority to be quoted as Jeremy Taylor or Bishop Hall or any of Escobar's twenty-four Elders.

The speaker recognizes that, while the truth of the "you" is more probable because more generally applicable, his own truth has some degree of probability. Escobar and Hall and Azor and Ames and the rest, in arguing toward the virtue of erstwhile sins, never go so far as to suggest that a particular act is *never* a sin; they merely say that in these severely restricted circumstances it is no sin. And here in this poem is the same movement: only in these circumstances may the "you" "Beg from above/A patterne of your love!" (ll. 44-45).

Donne's use of the image as an authority for making an exception to the general rule is, as has been said, similar to the casuists' use of opinions of "serious authorities." It may be, of course, difficult to see the distinction between an image which illuminates and an image employed as a statement of the special case. However, notice the use of the phoenix in this poem, which "hath more wit/By us, we two being one, are it" (ll. 23-24). The collapsing of distinctions between "we two" in the line into the "it" of the phoenix looks forward to the mystery at the end of the stanza. Insofar as "we two" are "it," the line defines the "being" of the speaker and his lover and consequently is a law governing their "proper act and end." As this law governs the two persons, and as they are not subject to those laws governing *separate* individuals, the line and the image contained in it become justification for their special case: "Wee dye and rise the same, and prove/Mysterious by this love" (ll. 26-27).

It is interesting to note the number of images in the *Songs and Sonets* which direct one toward the same concept and which are employed in the same way: "My face in thine eye, thine in mine appeares" ("The good-morrow," l. 15), is only one of dozens which suggest that "our two loves be one" ("The good-morrow," l. 20). In each case, the essential unity of the two lovers is asserted as a special case which denies the applicability of general law. Arguing against the fact of the human condition, the speaker of "A Valediction: forbidding mourning" insists that

> Our two soules therefore, which are one,
>   Though I must goe, endure not yet
> A breach, but an expansion,
>   Like gold to ayery thinnesse beate (ll. 21-24)

suggesting one "authority"; and then, to further support his argument, he suggests another: "If they be two, they are two so/As stiffe twin compasses are two" (ll. 25-26). The possibility of two souls "which are one" is an expression of a truth which Donne's speaker constantly employs to argue against the essential disjunction between persons. In "The Extasie," replete with images suggesting the same concept, one reads,

> When love, with one another so
>   Interinanimates two soules,
> That abler soule, which thence doth flow,
>   Defects of lonelinesse controules. (ll. 41-44)

The concept of union as a probable law of human behavior has been used by the speaker of this poem to argue against that which he accepts to be more probable: "defects of lonelinesse."

Ordinarily, in Donne's metaphors, a comparison is made which calls into question or seems to deny other truths. The suspension of an iron ball between two electromagnets is perfectly understandable when one recognizes the presence of those magnets, but at first glance it seems to deny our knowledge that all that goes up must come down. In short, one is astonished by the constant tendency among Donne's metaphors to deny what men know to be universally true. There is evidence here of Donne's assent to probabilism, and surely part of the response to Donne's metaphors derives from a knowledge that he has chosen to defend in the metaphor a truth which has less probability of truth than some other.

The effort on the part of the speaker to particularize his concept of his own situation is in reality an attempt to polarize as much as possible the difference of opinion between himself and the "you" of the poem. It is the same tendency as that of the casuists, and it comes out of the same necessity: it is only as one sees clearly the difference and the disagreement among laws that one is able to ascertain the truth with any certainty. The effort to polarize is not invidious, though it may be witty. The speaker, as he assents to a probable formulation of truth, knows that truth itself does exist and that conflict exists only among formulations of truth. If he, like the casuists, is to be both honest with himself and rigorous, he must discover the difference among formulations so that he may at the same time see the point at which they join. In *one* law, difference is unknown. Between *two* laws, difference must be not only noted but exaggerated. The speaker knows that it is mere sentimentality to assert that two truths, conflicting, are equally true and that one may without rigor choose between them as between peas. He knows it is invidious to act as if it does not matter which is the more true or the more applicable. He knows that even men of good-will may not merely be content with their choice of action. Truth matters, and mere goodwill is not enough. One must know and pursue to the end the consequences of moral choice.

Neither Donne's speaker nor the casuist is lazy. Neither man is willing to rest in an easy, or uneasy, skepticism. The speaker and the casuist are unwilling to be merely kind or merely to allow. They are unwilling to deny the real divisions among men. They know that there are men with knowledge as profound as theirs, with reasons as trained as theirs, with faith as deep, with verbal ability as facile, who still disagree with them.

We see then the speaker of these poems paying his interlocutor the high compliment of making clear for her, as well as for himself and for the reader, exactly how it is they disagree. The casuists are as rigorous. One is struck more by the disagreement among the laws—the rights of the rider opposed to the rights of the child in the way, the rights of the pursued as opposed to the rights of the unbaptized—than their agreement. As quoted earlier from *The Provincial Letters,* Pascal glee-fully points out the absurdity of Escobar's allowing a religious to leave off his habit when he goes to fornicate. Pascal and his readers are astonished by the suggestion that a religious would fornicate and that an elder of the Society of Jesus would entertain such a notion, but Pascal dissembles with his readers and they may with themselves.

It is the extreme case that produces the need for casuistry, the case that forces a man to choose between suicide and running down an innocent child in the highway. These choices are striking for they seem bizarre and decadent. Whether a child in the highway is baptized is an eccentric question. But surely, as the casuists pose these cases, as they force recognition of the extremity of the peculiarity, a more important fact emerges. There is no need to ask how one got into the extreme case, nor is there any need to ask why the rider is running from his pursuers. He is; men do, and they are faced with impossible choices, and it is sentimental to suggest that it is the *casuist* who is peculiar. *Men* are; and the casuist articulates that peculiarity by posing the extreme case.

The casuist does so by exaggerating the conflict among laws. As the casuist confronts the commandment "Thou shalt do no murder," he responds with the law which is most diametrically opposed, the law of self-defense. It is at the intersection of these two laws, where self-defense leads to murder, that the casuist finds his moral truth. One must then see clearly the ways the laws applicable to a certain case conflict so that one can see more clearly the precise point at which they join. As with two diameters drawn across a circle, one ascertains more clearly the center of the circle if their angle of intersection approaches ninety rather than zero degrees. At the point where laws most clearly contradict, they define truth.

Consider "The Flea." It is at the point where three different concepts governing their love cross one another that one discovers the truth toward which the speaker argues. In the first stanza, the image of the flea's biting him and her is employed to the point that sex is insignificant. In the second stanza, that insignificant bite has burgeoned to significance: "This flea is you and I, and this/Our mariage bed, and mariage temple is" (ll. 12-13). In the third stanza, the death of the flea has left "not thy selfe, nor mee the weaker now" (l. 24), and the method used by the poet's speaker is clear: each successive use of the image of the flea's bite has shifted in application. It is at the point where insignificance crosses significance that the "you" of the poem will be forced to submit to sex with the speaker. That is, it is at the point where the "you" of the poem can be forced to see that the flea's bite is insignificant by testing its significance, that the speaker's point may be won.

The disjunction here between "this, alas, is more then wee would doe" (l. 9) and "this/Our mariage bed, and mariage temple is" (ll. 12-13) is stressed. The speaker, like the casuists, places emphasis upon the dissimilarity of two views of a single subject in order to arrive at the possibility of a central truth. The separation is stressed precisely because there is no way to state the central truth directly. The force of the central truth is emphasized if it is limited by contradictions.

The wit in "The Expiration" arises out of the stark contrast between two opposing concepts. The poem, like others, is concerned with the moral implications of "this last lamenting kisse" (l. 1), and it ends with the admonition "Goe; and if that word have not quite kil'd thee,/Ease mee with death, by bidding mee goe too" (ll. 7-8). Contradictions abound in the poem: "Turne thou ghost that way, and let mee turne this" (l. 3), but contradictions began the poem. In the midst of a kiss, the speaker says, "So, so, breake off this last lamenting kisse" (l. 1), gently refusing to allow the kiss merely to die but wanting it to be cut off *in medias res*. Further, he does not want one or the other of them to send the other away: "We ask'd none leave to love; nor will we owe/Any, so cheape a death, as saying, Goe" (ll. 5-6). He wants them to break off the kiss in the middle and to turn away from each other at the same time: "Turne thou ghost that way, and let mee turne this,/And let our selves benight our happiest day" (ll. 3-4).

Yet the "you" of the poem has, between lines six and seven, not acceded to the speaker's request. She continues the kiss and forces him to action: *Goe*. The second stanza of the poem is the analysis of that admonition to action: the analysis is in three parts, and each of the parts is a formulation of a law governing their behavior. In line eight, we find the possibility that the effect of the word, her imminent death, leads him to despair: "Ease mee with death, by bidding mee goe too." But if the word has already taken its effect and she is dead, "let my word worke on mee,/And a just office on a murderer doe" (ll. 9-10). In the seventh and eighth lines, his own death is sought as an easement; in the ninth and tenth lines, it is a punishment. Yet, in the concluding lines of the poem, we find that "it be too late, to kill me so,/Being double dead, going, and bidding, goe" (ll. 11-12). Whatever happens to her as a result of his action, it is too late for her to take responsive action. He is already dead, leaving her and bidding her leave him. Each time the speaker has looked at the action, he has seen consequences which are in absolute contrast to one another, and the contrast is stressed. And it is at the point where execution and suicide and involuntary self-homicide join that the speaker discovers his truth.

When the speaker exaggerates the difference between himself and the "you" of the poems, he may separate himself from her in some honest or dishonest venture without that separation being final or total. All the speaker's assertions of their union are in fact true; he knows that he may go into Germany without a real separation, and he shows himself in these arguments to be able to disagree without either despair or skepticism.

The casuists always know that they may disagree with the law of God without disbelieving in his existence or his truth.

As the speaker of these poems goes about defending his private view, he resorts to law in the metaphor. There are very few poems in Donne's collection which are founded upon one metaphor, and the casuists themselves as they are moral theologians seem to be drawn toward collections in which they deal with a variety of cases and in each case refer to a variety of authorities. The application of *one* law to a case almost never exhausts the casuist's interest in his subject. It is the juxtaposition of cases and the variety of laws applicable to a case which provide much of the interest of the books of casuistry. It is possible and certainly necessary to investigate the manner in which metaphors are employed, that is, as they relate to one another and as they define and embody the central concept of the poem.

One notices immediately the tendency among the casuists to be inclusive in their citations of general principles. Escobar's putting together a "book" of moral theology and the titles of the collections of the seventeenth-century casuists indicate their desire: Perkins calls his book *The Whole Treatise of the Cases of Conscience,* indicating an attitude; and Jeremy Taylor says, in a passage already quoted, "Although I have not given answers to every doubt, yet have I told what we are to do when any doubt arises; I have conducted the doubting conscience by such rules which in all doubts will declare her duty" (p. xx). The books themselves tend toward inclusiveness, a tendency reinforced by the dictionary-like form of many of them, and the citations of authorities further reinforce that tendency. Any opinion of any authority that bears in the least way on the issue at hand is apposite and important.

A series of "questions" in Escobar's discussion of murder is illuminating: Question 39 is "Say that a soldier knows that he is fighting unjustly; may he nevertheless kill a soldier of the enemy army who rushes upon him to kill him?" Escobar continues: "May one kill an unjust aggressor upon the life of one's neighbor?" "Say that the person attacked gives up his rights?" "You have said that it is *permissible* to kill an unjust aggressor upon your life or that of your neighbor; I ask, are we *obliged* to do so?" "May one kill an attacker of one's possessions?" "May it be extended to members of a religious order, as these do not have any possessions of their own?" "I want to know of how great value a thing must be, for the saving of which I may kill a thief." "Is it permissible to kill a person attacking the property of one's neighbor?" "But is one obliged to do so?" (pp. 118-19).

The sequence of questions given here leads, of course, to Escobar's quotations from his twenty-four authorities, and the answers he gives are interesting as he makes his points and defines his distinctions; yet the questions themselves are of importance, for they indicate the movement of his thought as he progresses from part to part of the question, from self to neighbor, from life to goods. Unjust aggression in warfare has led him to unjust aggression in the private sector, first against life, his own and his neighbor's, then against goods, his own and his neighbor's. And he does not forget the distinction between permission for an act and obligation.

The inclusiveness here, in the casuist's practice, illuminates the poet's. In the poems there is an almost extravagant use of images. They pile upon one another with a sometimes breathtaking rapidity, and the need to accumulate images seems almost obsessive. The most famous example of this piling up of authorities is found in the third stanza of "The Canonization," where the speaker of the poem attempts to arrive at what he and his lover are made by love: "Call us what you will, wee are made such by love" (l. 19). In the next four lines, the speaker asserts that they are flies, tapers, the eagle and the dove, and the phoenix. This progression seems to move back and forth from one to two to one to two, and, in the one phoenix, "We two being one, are it," from one to two to one again. All bases in the progression of images seem to have been covered and, like Escobar's series of questions, the speaker pretends to catholicity.

Notice the ten lines beginning at the fifth stanza of "A Valediction: forbidding mourning."

> But we by a love, so much refin'd,
>   That our selves know not what it is,
> Inter-assured of the mind,
>   Care lesse, eyes, lips, and hands to misse.
>
> Our two soules therefore, which are one,
>   Though I must goe, endure not yet
> A breach, but an expansion,
>   Like gold to ayery thinnesse beate.
>
> If they be two, they are two so
>   As stiffe twin compasses are two. (ll. 17-26)

To be "inter-assured of the mind" is to find eyes, lips, hands unnecessary and irrelevant to one's union. But the quality of being "inter-assured of the mind" still admits of the expression "two soules" which must be forced into "which are one." And the breach—which is merely of bodies—is in that single soul an "expansion,/Like gold to ayery thinnesse beate." But the speaker attempts to confront all problems and says, "*If* they be two" (italics added), they are separate in this peculiarly identical fashion: "They are two so/As stiffe twin compasses are two."

The images frequently gain their effect by this accumulation. In "A Valediction: of weeping," we read,

> Let me powre forth
> My teares before thy face, whil'st I stay here,
> For thy face coines them, and thy stampe they beare,
> And by this Mintage they are something worth,
>   For thus they bee
>   Pregnant of thee;
> Fruits of much griefe they are, emblemes of more,
> When a teare falls, that thou falst which it bore,
> So thou and I are nothing then, when on a divers shore. (ll. 1-9)

The images of the stanza, coins, pregnant women, fruits, emblems are, in their progression, metaphors for the tears of the stanza; and one learns of the tears that they are coins *and* women *and* fruits *and* emblems. One senses that it is the mere exigency of the stanza form, the restriction of the nine-line stanza which prevents the speaker from extending his list, an extension which would bring him no closer to a definition of "tears" as he is now no farther from it with only four integers in the list.

The accumulation of images, like the accumulation of authorities, of course, arises out of the epistemology of both the speaker and the casuist. Neither believes the reason is capable of arriving at more than a very limited statement of truth. What is particular may be true; what is universal may be true. But as the particular truth mounts to universality, defects enter. One may achieve universality of truth, then, by accumulating particular truths. One cannot say what one is, if one is like the two lovers in "The Canonization" who prove mysterious. Yet one can say that, in a way, one is like flies and tapers and eagles and doves and phoenixes, and the accumulation of all of them leads toward a definition of the mystery that is the lovers. The concept "mystery" exists for the speaker as the concept "murder" exists for Escobar: neither can be defined *as it is*. They can only be defined as they show themselves in the particular situation. And the accumulation of all the particular situations—murder in defense of one's life, in defense of one's property, in defense of one's neighbor's life and property, and on and on—begins to mount to a definition of the concept *murder;* and it is a concept which cannot be defined in the abstract but which shows itself in certain limited ways in the concrete. As we see the poetry, we see an inability to trust the image to be expressive of particular truth. One could with profit compare Donne's apparent lack of confidence with Jonson's confidence. The very strenuousness of Donne's images implies an insecurity, as the strenuousness of the casuist's argument is surely indicative of his inability to believe that truth can be clearly stated.

There is also the assumption that truth may be gotten at, if not in *one clear word,* perhaps in the accumulation of a good many clear words. As the proliferation of law is necessary to get at the singularity of God's mind, so the proliferation of images, here, is expressive of the same kind of belief about method: not until one has before one the whole world does one have an understanding of the "government of things in God." The images attempt in their proliferation the evocation of that whole world: the more there are, the closer one comes to truth.

This accumulation of images is the method of enormously careful thinkers. All of the casuists are careful men. Thomas Pickering, speaking of William Perkins's knowledge of casuistry, says that it "could not be attained unto without great paines, much observation and long experience." Perkins himself agrees with the difficulty: "It is not a matter easy and at hand, but full of labour and difficulty: yea very large, like unto the maine sea: I will only (as it were, walke by the bankes of it, and propound the heads of doctrine, that thereby I may, at least, occasion others, to consider and handle the same more at large" (p. 3). Perkins is at one with everyone else in his admission of the largeness of the problem and the difficulty of solution.

After several pages of discussion and close reasoning, Ames admits in his discussion of an erroneous conscience that "no certaine and generall rule therefore can be set downe in this matter" (p. 11). Difficulty is always there and, though final solution of that difficulty is impossible, man must be extraordinarily careful. In his discussion of doubting conscience, Ames uses, on one page, the phrase "diligent care," and later he continues: "Using all diligence to be certaine (though we be not) it is lawful in many things to follow that opinion which is most probable" (p. 11). On the next page, Ames answers the question, "What shall one doe when his Conscience is doubtful?" "First, in all those doubts which doe any way belong to our practise, diligent enquiry is to be made, that we may clearly perceive the truth and not doubt." Further, he says of doubt, "One must labour diligently to *remove* these scruples, which reason can take away by due triall of the grounds of them" (p. 13).

In "Satyre III" Donne says:

> . . . On a huge hill,
> Cragged, and steep, Truth stands, and hee that will
> Reach her, about must, and about must goe;
> And what the hills suddennes resists, winne so;
> Yet strive so, that before age, deaths twilight,
> Thy Soule rest, for none can worke in that night.

To will, implyes delay, therefore now doe:
Hard deeds, the bodies paines; hard knowledge too
The mindes indeavours reach, and mysteries
Are like the Sunne, dazling, yet plaine to all eyes. (ll. 79-88)

The image of a person traveling around a mountain on a circular path, with each revolution coming closer and closer to the truth, is precisely illustrative of Donne's method in his poetry. Carefulness, energy, determination, the willingness to probe indefinitely will bring one to a truth which one cannot reach by direct apprehension.

As the speaker probes after truth by carefully accumulating image after image, each expressive of law, he juxtaposes those images in certain characteristic ways. There is, first, the mere listing of authorities, each one precisely supportive of the preceding one. This is a relatively infrequently used method, for one authority establishes the probable truth of an opinion, and there is no need for the citation of those authorities who agree. Accumulation adds no degree of probability. The sequence of images in the first stanza of "A Valediction: of weeping" would not have mounted to greater truth if the list had been greater, and the loss of understanding would have been negligible had the list been smaller.

On occasion, the casuists list the various opinions of the authorities in a different manner. On the question of just wars, Escobar has this to say: "Coninch asserts (quest. 4 #37) that it is impermissible to start a war if there is very little hope of victory. Cajetan requires virtual certainty of victory. But Palao (sec. 3 #17) thinks that probable certainty is sufficient. And Suarez (*On Charity* ch. 31 sec. 4) requires greater hope than the losses which are anticipated" (p. 124). Here four different opinions are given on the subject of just wars and the relation between the various opinions is that they are opposed as they all are brought to bear on the central question of the just war. Each is a different and equally probable explanation.

This more characteristic method of handling the image in the *Songs and Sonets* is for each image to be posed as an alternative to those images which preceded it. The sequence of images in the first stanza of "A Valediction: of weeping" is expressive of a single idea: their tears reflect each other. And when they are separated from one another "on a divers shore" (l. 9), "thou and I are nothing then" (l. 9). Yet posed, in the second stanza, is one image, of the tear as "all," drowned by other tears: "Till thy teares mixt with mine doe overflow/This world, by waters sent from thee, my heaven dissolved so" (ll. 17-18). This image is juxtaposed in such a way to the group of images of the first stanza as to be an alternative to them. In the first stanza tears had some importance insofar as they bore the stamp of the other's face: "And by this Mintage they are something worth" (l. 4). But, alternatively, the second stanza poses the destructive capability of the tears. The tears were "something worth" so long as they are together and facing one another; but, at the same time, they are destructive of the two so long as they are together and facing one another. The second stanza is posed as an alternative view of the central image of the first stanza. It is as if the speaker said, *This thing is true, but, if you cannot accept it, this other thing is equally true.* The distinction made between the former and the latter posited statements is that the former may be totally inapplicable, and, if so, the latter must be applicable. It should be noted that the circumstances of the two stanzas shift and that, in the circumstances of the second stanza, the first becomes untrue.

The question posed in the poem "A Valediction: of weeping" is, *Should we weep?* and the first and second stanzas, in their images, give alternative answers. The images are juxtaposed to one another in such a way as to imply a contradiction, but, because circumstances, defined in the image itself, have changed, there is no contradiction. This use of image sequences is frequently found in the *Songs and Sonets.* The shift from the beaten gold image in "A Valediction: forbidding mourning" to "If they be two, they are two so . . ." (l. 25) is characteristic. The former image is posed, and the latter is suggested as alternative, depending on circumstance.

When the casuists suggest an alternative opinion about a question, they do not thereby reject or imply rejection of the former opinion. Both are equally probable depending on how one sees one's circumstances. In like manner, the speaker suggests one possibility and then another, and, while the two possibilities are contradictory and cannot exist at the same time with respect to the central issue, neither the speaker nor the casuist forces a choice between them. Circumstances alter cases.

This posing of alternatives, a favored ploy of both Donne's speaker and the casuists, is effective because it appears to leave the doubting conscience or the "you" of the poem with no choice of action except to do what had seemed impermissible. Although the alternatives appear to conflict, they both justify the same action. The authorities cited by Escobar in the passage already quoted appear to give different views on the question of starting a just war. Yet all four opinions allow the war, though under different circumstances, and all four opinions are united in their opposition to the assertion that no war is just. In like manner, when Donne's speaker poses alternatives, he does so in such a way as to maintain his opposition to the "you" of the poem. As he shifts from *one* to *two* when he moves from the image of gold to the image of compass legs, he only *appears* to pose them as alternatives. Both images support his contention that there is no disunion between lovers.

There is a third method in which the image is used in these poems. Here, the sequence of images builds, the first leading into the second, the second into the third, the third into the fourth; each time the central truth is more and more clearly restricted. A good example of this method from among the casuists is Escobar's case on murder and the nightrider, already referred to frequently in this study.

Leaving aside the astonishing ability of the rider to tell from horseback at some speed and distance whether a child is unbaptized, one sees the relationships among the authorities and opinions and laws which Escobar poses. Each restricts more than the last. There are several laws brought to bear on this case: one has a right to flee a pursuer, one has the right to use public highways, one must be careful of the rights of others to use public highways, one must always give up one's own baptized life when one has a choice between that life and an unbaptized one. As long as the person in the way is baptized and as long as the other uses certain "circumspection," the rider may with impunity run him down and kill him. At the intersection of all these laws, truth is found; and if, from this vantage point, the intersection of all these laws results in an impasse, that need not be a concern here. The method of argument is the concern. One acts only at the point and in the way that is permissible according to *every* law. And the progression of laws in the argument is ordered around the point of agreement of the laws.

Between lines forty-nine and sixty-eight of "The

Extasie" there is a series of metaphors which are argued in just this manner. There appear here to be five related metaphors, each of which more and more clearly circumscribes the circumstances under which it would be right for the two persons of the poem to mount beyond the ecstasy of the first forty-eight lines of the poem to a greater and more complete ecstasy of the souls and bodies. As the metaphors accumulate, each one expressive of a different but related law of behavior, it becomes more and more clear that the only course of action left to the two persons is just that movement toward the bodies.

After the question posed in lines forty-nine and fifty, we have the argument: "They are ours, though they are not wee, Wee are/The intelligences, they the spheare" (ll. 51-52), which defines the law expressing the relationship between the spheres and the intelligences which govern them: the spheres belong to the intelligences but are not synonymous with them. There is explicitly here the assumption that the intelligences "owe" the spheres some duty, the spheres being unable to continue in their promised rounds without a governing intelligence.

The next metaphor, that of an alloy's strengthening and making useful a pure metal being like the bodies' relation to the souls, suggests a different relationship from the preceding one. The intelligences had an apparent duty to perform with respect to the spheres, but, in themselves, were complete without the spheres. Here, the pure metal—possibly gold—is of value only as the alloy yields its "forces, sense, to us" (l. 55). The alloy is not dross, it is necessary to the employment of the metal, and consequently the metal owes the alloy "thankes" (l. 53).

The next metaphor defines in a more complex manner the relation between the body and the soul:

> On man heavens influence workes not so,
>   But that it first imprints the ayre,
> Soe soule into the soule may flow,
>   Though it to body first repaire. (ll. 57-60)

A paraphrase of this passage runs something like the following: heaven's influence on man works through the medium of air, and in that medium the incorporeal soul has access to other souls, even though the body is its natural home. If this can be accepted, we have a law governing the relative positions of heaven's influence, souls and bodies. Heaven's influence works naturally through the medium of air, a medium also available to the soul as it moves out from the body; but the medium of air as an avenue for the soul is not its natural medium: "it to body first repaire" (l. 60). The body is the soul's natural medium, though it may employ others. The progression to this metaphor is clear. Intelligences "owned" spheres and consequently have a duty to direct their motions; pure metal is made useful by the addition of alloy and therefore owes that alloy "thankes"; heaven's influence can be felt *only* as it functions through the air; and, in a like manner, the soul, while having a choice of air and body, functions most naturally through the bodies. The important word in this metaphor is "imprints" (l. 58), a notion suggested in the first metaphor, in the direction of the spheres' movement by the intelligences, and in the second in the notion of metal being made useful. The sequence of concepts builds to this word "imprints," and we understand by it that heaven's influence is made visible and viable only as it is imprinted upon the palpable substance *air*. The relationship between soul and body in this sequence of metaphors has been gradually restricted to the point that souls are important only as they stamp themselves upon bodies.

The speaker next defines the relation between body and soul even more strictly:

> As our blood labours to beget
>   Spirits, as like soules as it can,
> Because such fingers need to knit
>   That subtile knot, which makes us man. (ll. 61-64)

Here the relation between body and soul is seen more clearly. The effort of the blood to "beget" spirits like souls, this apparent "law" of the behavior of blood, is for the first time posited; and one knows for the first time that, as blood labors to "beget" spirits, the body labors to seize the soul and that whatever the drive of the souls toward the bodies, whatever impulse there is downward to bodies, there is a like impulse upward toward souls: "Because such fingers need to knit/That subtile knot, which makes us man" (ll. 63-64). For the first time, in this metaphor, the relationship of the body and soul has been considered from the point of view of the body, and for the first time the body is seen—in the blood—attempting to tie itself to the soul. The relationship in the metaphor is absolutely equal; it is a "knot" of equal-sized ropes which joins the two. Furthermore, the knot is that "which makes us man," and the relationship between body and soul has been dealt with from a new perspective: the bodies are no longer owned; they join with the soul in an endeavor in which they face one another with equality. And the joint endeavor is that "which makes us man" (l. 64). Only insofar as the body and the soul join together in this equal state is *man* created.

The final metaphor of the series is that in which the soul, said to be the "great Prince," lies imprisoned unless it is freed by being loosed into the body.

> So must pure lovers soules descend
>   T'affections, and to faculties,
> Which sense may reach and apprehend,
>   Else a great Prince in prison lies. (ll. 65-68)

The equality between the body and the soul, posed in the preceding metaphor, is here altered: only through the body can the soul gain freedom. The body is given all the importance here, all the power and strength, all the ability to *act*, which the soul had been given earlier; and, far from being mere alloy or sphere or medium of air or even the fingers of one hand as opposed to the fingers of another, the body is here given the importance of that which *frees*. It is only as the body is present and surrounding the soul that the soul is freed of its incapacity and may then act.

In an interesting way, these four lines suggest spatial movement of the souls which at first supports and then undercuts our expectations. "So must pure lovers soules *descend*" (l. 65, italics added) brings one back to traditional, conventional territory, where bodies exist *beneath* souls as spheres exist beneath intelligences and as air exists beneath heaven; yet the movement *downward* to bodies is a movement *outward* toward freedom. It is a reversal of what is expected, and the subliminal image is clear: the prince must go down into the stairways and passageways beneath the prison tower, into the public rooms and courts where free men move and the business of the kingdom is transacted. This whole movement *down* to affections and to faculties, reinforced by the verb, suggests the ability of the body to act, and it is action which frees.

The concluding line of this series of metaphors, "To'our bodies turne wee then" (l. 69), is prepared for and proved by the series of conceits which precede it.

The *necessity* for returning to the bodies is prepared for and even demanded by this series of conceits. And each of them, as they apply to the central issue, the relationship of the souls to the bodies, restricts more and more and requires more and more the final movement. As intelligences have a duty to spheres, as metal needs its alloy, as heaven's influence needs its medium of air, as one hand needs another to knit knots, as princes need to be freed from prisons, the soul needs its body.

These metaphors are not posed as alternatives to one another, nor is each one simply added to the other as one more supportive illustration of what it is the speaker tries to say. The variety of metaphors in the series has, in the one to the other, a tangential relationship. Souls "owe" something to bodies, but, at the same time, they need bodies as metal needs alloy; they are at home in the medium of the bodies, and yet there is the knowledge that, if they are not at home there, they are imprisoned; and, above all, the relationship between body and soul has all the equality of one hand knitting a fist with the other hand, five fingers intermingled with five fingers, indistinguishable.

A variety of laws is faced here, no one of which is apparently fully applicable and each one of which is, at the least, partially contradictory of some of the others. It is of course impossible for the "law" governing the relationship of intelligences to spheres to be fully applicable to a situation if the law governing the relationship of princes to prisons is at the same time applicable. And both deny the validity of the law governing the knitting of hands, five fingers to five fingers. Yet at the point where all conjoin, truth is found. The second builds upon the first, the third upon the second, until there is no room left but that area which is defined as *truth* for the speaker.

The method of casuistry is a neutral tool necessary to one who chooses to see his situation in moral terms. It may be employed for the purposes of satire, humor, sheer fun—as well as for the resolution of what is ordinarily considered to be moral doubt. Critics of casuistry are generally shocked by the conclusions reached in the cases. One is taken by the moral obtuseness of Escobar's having said one could murder a thief who came to rob one of one gold sovereign. The science of moral theology seems, in that case, to have taken leave of reason and married itself to late decay. Yet the process of reasoning which leads Escobar to assert such an opinion allows the poet opportunity for displays of wit, and, if the method of reasoning seems to be no longer useful, in the opinion of some, for the resolution of moral doubt, Donne shows that it is enormously useful in the witty argument between lovers.

While the Protestants and the Jesuits are alike, essentially, in their method of argument and while the differences between them are only those of degree, it is the Jesuits whose method is closest to Donne's poetry. The Jesuits appear to have taken the method of reasoning to its extreme; they are the most indulgent and, consequently, the most shocking and, paradoxically, the most rigorous in their reasoning. Had Donne read Escobar's cases, one can imagine a part of the man responding with real distaste; but surely another part of the man would have gleefully fastened onto the trope as ideally suited to poetry. The more shocking the reasoning of the case of conscience, the more similar it seems to become to the poems of the *Songs and Sonets*.

The conclusions of these cases and these poems are the more shocking as they are recognized to be moral truths, for what is recognized in them is not what is complacently seen to be *moral*. Yet truth, as it is moral, is paradoxical in the cases and in the poems; and it expresses for the speaker and for the doubting conscience, if for no one else, their "proper act and end." The *yes* which is the answer to these moral questions reverberates with truths far more pervasive than *it is permissible to flee or to fornicate or to fight off an attacker*. That *yes* places the doubting conscience within the structure of the world and beyond the conflict of law and the disjunction between the one and the many. The *yes* for the speaker is an assent to both the variety and the unity of life, and it expresses an assent to a truth which is nonverbal, a truth which, like the sea, is vast and all encompassing and which, beyond understanding, can only be experienced. Perkins said of his subject that it was "very large, like unto the maine sea" (p. 3), and Taylor said, "Whatsoever swims upon any water, belongs to this exchequer" (p. xv).

Moral ends, for the seventeenth century, precede ascetic ends, as rectitude precedes holiness; and behind every argument in the books of cases and in the cases of the poems is this assumption: the discovery of moral truth is the discovery of some small part of final truth, and the *yes* to the act is an assent to that limitless truth. It is a discovery of the truth about the self, about man's "proper act and end"; and, as it is so, the interstices between and among the patterned and reticulated laws and self are filled in, and the casuist joins himself to the world in a union which is seamless and whole.

V

The Sound of the Speaker's Voice

When the speaker says, "When my grave is broke up againe" ("The Relique," l. 1), with his bizarre prediction and even more bizarre confidence, one knows that one is in the presence of a special mind and voice, whose tone is noticed before other things, a tone dependent upon and a result of so many considerations that, while it is noticed first, it is understood last. The speaker is a doubting conscience, and the contradiction inherent in the phrase suggests the contradictions in the speaker himself. As the nature of the doubting conscience is understood—his assent to a truth which is at once accessible and inaccessible, his method of reasoning which may be neither methodical nor reasonable—the resonance of his voice, his attitude toward what he says, toward the "you" of the poems, himself, and his achievement in the poems, are more clearly understood.

The speaker is seldom serene. Even in so quiet a poem as "The Relique," the speaker's voice comes to us charged with expectancy and conflict:

> When my grave is broke up againe
> Some second ghest to entertaine,
> (For graves have learn'd that woman-head
> To be to more then one a Bed)
>   And he that digs it, spies
> A bracelet of bright haire about the bone. . . . (ll. 1-6)

The violence of "broke up againe" is repeated in the images "digs" (l. 5) and "digges" (l. 14) and reflected in "Comming and going" (l. 27). The speaker imagines himself dead and buried, but the vision has no calmness about it, and the absence of life is here no end to activity. "The Relique" indicates a quality which is found throughout the collection. There is no stasis, and the speaker is most aware of, most sensitive to movement, activity, conflict. Rest and peace do not figure at all as he presents himself in the poems.

This inability of the speaker to rest and be easy, even in death, shows itself most clearly in the poems in mental activity. The speaker cannot stop thinking. In each of the first two stanzas of "The Relique," the grave is "broke up againe" (l. 1), and one senses that the speaker's mind, once attached to its subject, is unable to let go. Once the conceit presents itself to the speaker, and once his mind begins to analyze the conceit, momentum carries him forward as much as do the requirements of logic. He is compelled to think. The speaker's mind seems to have a movement of its own irrespective of the subject which confronts it. The first four lines of the second stanza illustrate the point:

> If this fall in a time, or land,
> Where mis-devotion doth command,
> Then, he that digges us up, will bring
> Us, to the Bishop, and the King. (ll. 12-15)

One notices the addition of "or land," and "and the King" and "and some men" (l. 19). It is not immediately obvious why these phrases are in the lines, but one does recognize a compulsion in the speaker's voice: his mind, closing in on its subject, is unable to cease its analysis. He goes beyond the ordinary requirements of logical discourse, and, arguing with the "you," may have convinced her before he convinces his own doubting conscience.

As the speaker argues, he moves from one concept to another with only the barest suggestion of their connection. The first four lines suggest the pattern. The first two assert a fact about graves: they entertain guests, one after another after another. The second two lines, enclosed significantly in parentheses, assert that graves have learned from womanhood how "to be to more then one a Bed." The three integers of comparison are alike: graves and beds admit of successive occupants, and, as womanhood is located here in the vagina, womanhood too admits of successive occupants. But the point of the comparison is lost and is not discovered in the poem but in the speaker's mind. The comparison tells less about graves than about the kind of sensibility the speaker of these poems has. The association of graves with vaginas is excursive and suggests that the speaker speaks without consideration for his listener. He appears more concerned with satisfying his own need for the excursion than with whether he is understood. In fact, although he is arguing with another person, he seems not to be aware of how that other person receives what he says. His mind, despite the range of his ideas and the catholicity of his interests, is directed inward, and his voice seems to listen to itself and to respond to itself and to use the response of the "you" only as fresh impetus to new flights of fancy.

For example, the first stanza of "The Relique" is a fairly conventional statement for a man with poetic ability. Aside from the sudden illuminations of certain phrases and the strange insertion of lines three and four, there is nothing here to suggest eccentricity of mind; and the response of the "you" implicit after that stanza is an easy *Surely so*. Yet the speaker moves from that response to an extravagance: the second stanza is a more bizarre and exotic statement of the first. It is as if the speaker refuses to recognize limits to logical discourse. Bracelets, suggesting lovers, also suggest relics; and, if one may admire ordinary lovers, one must worship extraordinary ones. The speaker seems intent on telling all, even if that all seems too much, irrelevant to his concerns, confusing, and contradictory.

This extravagance is not of the imagination, though that is part of it. It is an extravagance of the reason, an extravagance seen clearly in the concluding lines of the second stanza:

> All women shall adore us, and some men;
> And since at such time, miracles are sought,
> I would have that age by this paper taught
> What miracles wee harmelesse lovers wrought. (ll. 19-22)

There is a dogmatism, an extreme and positive certainty of the mind in these lines which suggests an attitude of the speaker toward the reason. In *"all* women shall adore" (italics added) the speaker's tendency toward the absolute statement is seen, a tendency which he himself undercuts and mocks by the succeeding phrase, "some men" (l. 19). This tendency to the extreme statement and the equal tendency to undercut that statement suggest that the reason is not employed in these poems merely to convince; it does not merely perform its specified function of leading to certifiably true conclusions; it is a medium of self-expression and self-investigation for the speaker. Certainly the "you" listens to the speaker, and as certainly we listen to him. But we know that, most of all, the speaker listens to himself.

The reader recognizes the intensity with which the speaker speaks. He seems driven to say what he does say, to argue in the way he argues, and that drive only begins with the conflict between himself and the "you" of these poems. It is only as she points out to him a conflict which he recognizes as real that he argues; yet the resulting argument is only partially an attempt to convince her. Beginning with the conflict between himself and the "you" of the poem, the argument moves quickly forward to the more important issue: the speaker's own conception of truth. The truth he seeks in this poem is, minimally, a truth which has to do with the bracelet itself and its importance. But the truth of the bracelet is suggestive of other truths which have to do with the nature of their love for one another and of truths which have to do with their "proper act and end." It is these more important truths which introduce confusion and make for doubt in the mind of the speaker; and as the speaker himself is unsure of his truths, he argues to convince himself as much as or more than to convince the "you" of the poem. The intensity with which the speaker responds to the "you" is a result of the intensity with which the speaker responds to the problem of moral truth. The "you" in any poem may point out to the speaker that he is wrong, that the bracelet is merely a bracelet and that the speaker errs in placing such emphasis and importance upon it. That it is *she* who does so is of course important. But her assertion of something he also recognizes as truth throws the problem back on the speaker of the poems, makes the problem an internal one, and makes the manner of his argument more intense as the conflict is the more localized. What *he* thinks about the bracelet is as much or more at issue than what he is able to convince her to think about the bracelet.

This is not to say that the speaker of these poems does not care about the "you," in the argument or in love. He apparently cares about her as intensely as he cares about his own soul. As he argues, he argues with himself and then turns to her for response or approval. He argues to convince himself—and he does so in her presence. Surely implicit in these comments is the assumption that, while conflict exists between the speaker and the "you" of the poem, that conflict is a public manifestation of the internal conflict: the doubting conscience. And, as the "you" attacks the speaker on one or another moral ground, she merely articulates for the reader and for the speaker a problem the speaker already confronts.

Consequently, at least one of the reasons for the intensity of the argument in the poems is seen. The speaker does not need to convince the *reader* nor does he have to argue at such lengths and at such complexity to convince the "you." The readers and the "you" are not nearly so much as the speaker doubting consciences. They have not had his experience and do not have his doubt and did not recognize the moral problem until it was pointed out for them. Their consciences are peripheral to his concerns, for it is his own soul with which he is taken. The speaker listens to his own voice with fascination as great as his audience's.

This inward-looking quality in the poems, a quality most clearly there in those poems whose dramatic setting is, ironically, the most clear, suggests an insecurity in the speaker which is everywhere apparent and which is shown in the lengths to which he feels he must go in supporting his argument, in the intensity and complexity of that argument, in the dramatic force which he gives to each supportive statement. He protests far too much, and it is clear that one of the persons he is attempting to convince is his own doubting conscience.

In the kind of world in which the speaker finds himself, this insecurity is a natural reaction. The world does not show itself, and, while laws are evident everywhere, the applicability of those laws to one's own situation is nowhere clear. The speaker knows himself to be an anomaly. His response to this uncertainty is often strident. It is as if, in the rapidity of his thought and the forcefulness of his images, he has abandoned the attempt to convince in favor of the attempt to overwhelm. The reasoning seems too close to be right, and one suspects that the speaker is not being totally honest.

There is a duplicity in the speaker. Clearly, in some of the poems, the speaker toys with his interlocutor, arguing with her over matters which finally do not matter, employing arguments whose truth and relevance rest upon his ability to assert them and not upon any intrinsic worth. Those poems are games which the speaker plays. But this sense of duplicity spills over into even the most solemn of poems and the most grave of matters:

> When my grave is broke up againe
> Some second ghest to entertaine,
> (For graves have learn'd that woman-head
> To be to more then one a Bed). (ll. 1-4)

The speaker is unable to be less than witty, unable to suggest a concept without, in a fugal manner, giving the same concept again in a different key. The shift in tone from the first two lines to the third and fourth lines, the shift from relative solemnity to cynical, humorous sexuality, implies an inability to commit himself to the one or the other; and the forcefulness of the metaphor only appears to belie the indecisiveness of the speaker.

The electricity of the wit covers up what has not been recognized so clearly before: the speaker is a doubting conscience, and his wit is not merely a response to that doubt but is also an expression of it. At least one of the loci of the wit in the poems is the perplexity among words; the speaker employs words in such a way as to increase the sense of the disjunction between them: "A bracelet of bright haire about the bone." The *b* sounds and the circle of the bracelet link together bone and hair, whose texture could not be in greater contrast. As the speaker suggests the hard, dry whiteness of the bone circled about by soft, shining, yellow hair, the glitter against the flat, smooth bone, the effects he achieves are consequences of the nervous play of his mind over the multifarious sensations of the universe. They are not consequences of a mind driving single-mindedly toward its goal. In these juxtapositions of disparate sensations and ideas there is a hesitancy on the speaker's part to commit himself to one concrete thing, and there is a constant tendency to pull back and restate things in other ways. The duplicity in the poems is of a very special kind. The speaker frequently says what he may not believe to be true, and the second stanza of "The Relique" is a prime example, the tone of the stanza being daring and playful. But he believes he *must* speak in this manner. His refusal to commit himself to one concept is repeated here in his refusal to commit himself to one tone. There is always a sense that the speaker will assert something and will defend that assertion to the furthest limits of logic and rhetoric without believing that the assertion has more than a limited truth.

As one listens to the *Songs and Sonets,* one senses that the speaker knows too much, his mind is too catholic for his own ease, that the very range of his ideas and understandings and knowledges forces him to express that range in his conversation with the "you," an expression that complicates his love for her and that makes impossible a more simple response to her. He is trapped by his mind, and his discomfort transmits itself in the degree of his energy and the intensity of his investigations into the reasons for doubt. In "The Relique," for example, the speaker, attempting to use the bracelet as a means of delivering a compliment to the "you," cannot forget, even as he begins his compliment, the sinister and sexy thought, "(For graves have learn'd that woman-head/To be to more then one a Bed)" (ll. 3-4). He is aware of the resurrection of the bodies and the union of the souls with the bodies on Judgment Day. And, in the second stanza, theology leads the speaker to canon law and the recognition of relics by ecclesiastical and secular authorities. Those thoughts lead the speaker, more deeply, into the moral history of man: "Our hands ne'r toucht the seales,/Which nature, injur'd by late law, sets free" (ll. 29-30). The burden of the speaker's knowledge almost overwhelms the compliment of the poem; and, while that knowledge is surely to be employed in the speaker's drive toward truth, it is also to be *overcome* in his compliment to the "you." His knowledge, like the knowledge of the moral theologians generally, complicates his response to his situation. Only as Escobar recognized that one must consider whether a baby is baptized did he doubt. Donne's speaker here shows the same complex response.

The speaker's thought is then at once the hindrance to an easy access to both his life and the "you" and also the only means to that access. Consequently, the poems focus on the processes of the speaker's mind to a degree unmatched elsewhere in the lyric. Like a man crossing sheets of ice, the speaker watches his feet, knowing that the next step in his progress may be the last before disaster and yet certainly the only means to safety. The speaker's thought is synonymous with his emotion, and the disjunction between the two concepts is a verbal one. The speaker's thought is the action on which the poems concentrate. The sound of the speaker's voice supports such a contention. When the first stanza is heard, with its variety of independent and subordinate clauses, its parentheses, its appositional phrases, a man's mind shows itself continuously active and alive. The speaker's mind and voice run on and on and the complexity of thought, like the complexity of syntax, is dizzying. His mind is charged with energy. Other poets, such as Milton, are equally energetic, but that energy expresses itself in his poems with a more singular effect; that is, the mind of Milton's speaker shows itself to be more focused and more able to shut out variety. Donne's speaker's mind thrives on variety. And the focus of the poems is on the speaker's perception of that variety. He seems most to need to say everything at once, to get it all into one sentence, and occasionally even into one image.

The nervous energy in the poems, the sense that the speaker's mind is jumping from one concept to another to another, and the brilliance of that movement dismay the reader. And the exhilaration at the end of one of these poems is qualified by exhaustion. This kind of genius neither soothes nor comforts. It is too special and too inward-looking. One wonders why the man may not be more like other people, more ordinary, easier on one's sensibilities and less demanding. One does not know, of course, what the speaker is like in other circumstances, for his voice is heard only when he confronts the "you" in one of these brilliant and triumphant displays of wit and learning. But in these circumstances the speaker demands more of the reader than he wants to give, precisely because the speaker sees so very much being demanded of himself and his mind. The speaker is besieged, but not merely by the "you." His own knowledge, like that of the doubting conscience, destroys his security. One recognizes the speaker's private ironies. Of course, the speaker mocks his readers and, in a way, himself, for they have wanted things to be simpler than they are, less complex, less opaque to the sensibilities and reason. He mocks that need, showing that in these circumstances simplicity is sentimentality and that one arrives at truth only as one is willing to be special—in the intricacy of one's reasoning and the catholicity of one's perceptions. Even at his most triumphant, the speaker convinces the "you" of these poems in a lonely way.

One suspects finally that irony is directed toward the nature of the speaker's own learning; it is an irony shared by the "you" of the poem and by the reader, if he chooses. For the speaker recognizes that all his learning and all his verbal ability mount to the conclusion that learning is insufficient, and wit leads to an epistemological and moral despair, if he and the "you" of the poems do not agree to stop this side of that line. The cutting edge of the poetry is turned inward, and, at least from the reader's point of view, lays the speaker barer than the speaker may intend. Casuistry, except in the most myopic of cultures, has always had the same effect. Even as one recognizes the legitimacy of the effort of casuistry, one's need for it lays bare the moral precariousness of one's situation.

The assertion at the end of "The Relique" mounts above these considerations:

> . . . but now alas,
> All measure, and all language, I should passe,
> Should I tell what a miracle shee was. (ll. 31-33)

The achievement of the lines is the greater because of the difficulty of arriving at them. They arise out of no calm assertion of truths and from no clear, logical pro-gressions. The assertion of mysteries—and what must be seen as the proof of those mysteries—is all the greater because the speaker had, with such abandon, led one to expect that there is no mystery, only conflict, no mira-cle, only cynicism.

The speaker has courage. He is not willing to decide a priori that a bit of learning is irrelevant or that some fact, conflicting with what he wants to prove, should be suppressed. Not only is all knowledge grist for his mill; his mill must accept all that is forced upon it. He admits the similarity between graves and beds and womanheads even if that similarity is discordant and even if its import is unclear. And, as he accepts it, he turns it to his own uses, showing that the "miracle shee was" (l. 33) is more clearly miraculous when one sees those discordant possibilities.

This courage is no less than the faith found in the writings of the moral theologians. The speaker of these poems and the casuists both finally assert the possibility of miracles—even the miracle of escaping from doubt into certainty. In their argument, the speaker and the "you" of these poems have committed themselves, be-hind the tension of their argument and beyond their skepticism, to a faith in the existence and the final—if not the immediate—accessibility of truth. In that belief, if in few others, the speaker and his lover rest serenely.

VI

The Mind of the Poet

Conscience is a function of the practical intellect.
It is the mind of man passing moral judgments.
                                                    McAdoo, p. 66

The mind of the casuist has a different cast from others
of the same period and even from those with the same
kind of education. The casuist is a skeptic, but his faith
separates him from classical skepticism. He believes in
the efficacy of reason, but he is willing to do violence to
reason to make his point. He is practical to the point of
being pedestrian, but his effort is directed toward ulti-
mate things. He seeks to define, but his effort is not
primarily intellectual. His work is occasional, but he is
concerned with final religious truth. He gives the appear-
ance in his book of quibbling, but his work is charged
with moral intensity.

The impulse toward casuistry is predicated upon
occasion. The occasions which demand casuistry do not
happen to young men only, confronting their young
women, nor do they occur only in the lives of the witty
or the gravely solemn. They occur frequently and ran-
domly, and, as they do, those occasions make those who
respond to them seem kin. Donne's speakers employ the
casuistical method, not because it is their only mode of
expression, but because it is peculiarly suited to the

occasion in which the speakers sometimes find them-
selves: they confront a listener who has questioned on
moral grounds their actions. Faced with that fact, they
employ casuistry, and this is true whether the speaker is
a young man, an old one, confronting his God or his
mistress, whether he is solemn or playful. The analysis
of the casuistry of the *Songs and Sonets* in the preced-
ing chapters of this study has perhaps implied that
Donne's interest in casuistry and his use of the mode
was limited to those intense and worldly poems. The
casuistry of the *Songs and Sonets* is repeated in the
casuistry of the rest of Donne's canon, whether poetry
or prose, and it is the *practical intellect* which is most
often engaged when Donne confronts the world about
him.

In a quite fantastic letter written during the sum-
mer of 1610, Donne attempts a compliment to Miss
Bridget White and bases the compliment on the conceit
of her having *left* his environs:

Madame,
I could make some guesse whether souls that go to heaven, retain
any memory of us that stay behinde, if I knew whether you ever
thought of us, since you enjoyed your heaven, which is your self,
at home. Your going away hath made *London* a dead carkasse. A
Tearm, and a Court do a little spice and embalme it, and keep it
from putrefaction, but the soul went away in you: and I think
the onely reason why the plague is somewhat slackned, is, be-
cause the place is dead already, and no body left worth the
killing. Wheresoever you are, there is *London* enough: and it is a
diminishing of you to say so, since you are more then the rest of
the world. When you have a desire to work a miracle, you will
return hither, and raise the place from the dead, and the dead
that are in it; of which I am one, but that a hope that I have a
room in your favour keeps me alive; which you shall abundantly
confirme to me, if by one letter you tell me, that you have
received my six; for now my letters are grown to that bulk, that I

may divide them like *Amadis* the *Gaules* book, and tell you, that
this is the first letter of the second part of the first book.
Strand S. Peters   *Your humblest, and affectionate*
   day at nine.   *servant,* J.D.

(Bald, pp. 186-87)

Characteristically, the departure of Miss White from
London has led the poet into the initial question of the
relationship between souls and the memory, and that
question for Donne is founded upon the moral state-
ment: her departure has made London a dead carcass.
The letter, the compliment embodied there, and the
initial theological question—all are founded upon the
moral question stated, elaborated, and answered in the
central part of the letter. The writer is not simply able
to compliment his lady; he must justify her against what
he himself knows to be her sin, and his method is to
posit the sin first, then to move on to justification.

In the letter "To the Countesse of Bedford (Honour
is so sublime perfection)" we see the same effort, where
the speaker's attempts to pay honor to the lady give
way to a statement of why she deserves no honor at all,
and the remainder of the poem is an argument against
that statement: "You teach . . . a thing unknowne/To
our late times, the use of specular stone,/Through which
all things within without were shown" (ll. 28-30). There
was of course no reason for the speaker to compare the
lady to God in the opening lines of the poem in order
merely to compliment her. He chooses to do so to
compliment her the more, as it arises out of a disadvan-
tageous position.

We see the same effort among the elegies. In "The
Autumnall," the speaker astonishingly compares an ag-
ing woman to a young one to the detriment of the
young one. The speaker asserts, in the face of most

experience, "Yong *Beauties* force our love, and that's a
Rape,/This doth but *counsaile,* yet you cannot scape"
(ll. 3-4). The whole effort of the poem is in line five
when the speaker says, "If t'were a *shame* to love, here
t'were no *shame,*" where the speaker declares his doubt
and the normal reason for it. The intensity of "The
Autumnall" comes out of this man's insisting that the
autumn is, after all, better than springtime, that spring-
time is, despite what everybody knows, mere prologue
to reality. This man does not hedge the issue by saying
that youth is good for some and age good for others:
youth is good only for those whose taste still pants after
ephemeral things; but the speaker's love is such that

> Since such loves naturall lation is, may still
>   My love descend, and journey downe the hill,
> Not panting after growing beauties, so,
>   I shall ebbe out with them, who home-ward goe. (ll. 47-50)

The serene satisfaction of these lines is achieved at some
cost, for they assert a special truth whose weight has to
be demonstrated, not merely announced.

   Even in "Elegie XIX," the speaker lying naked in
bed seems more aware of that which resists him and
which resists his desire than that which supports him:
"The foe oft-times having the foe in sight,/Is tir'd with
standing though he never fight" (ll. 3-4). The successive
images of the poem all point toward the variety of
defenses with which a woman may gird herself: *girdle,
breastplate, lace, busk, gown, coronets, shoes, white
robes.* The speaker is aware of that against which he
must argue, and his effort is to come to new and special
truths surmounting old: "To teach thee, I am naked
first; why than/What needst thou have more covering
then a man" (ll. 47-48). The poems, almost all of them,

whether or not included in the *Songs and Sonets* are meant for just this purpose, *to teach,* and in that they are moral. If the teaching in some of them is *to be naked second,* we need not tarry over that thought, for in all of them the speaker teaches something, even if the subject be sex or the pupil be God.

When a man cries out, "Batter my heart, three person'd God; for, you/As yet but knocke, breathe, shine, and seeke to mend" (ll. 1-2), he is now arguing with his God and even preaching to his God in the same manner he had argued with the woman who had shared his bed or his table or his life. The speaker's confrontation with her prepared him and sharpened his wit for this confrontation with his triune God in this religious poem. In the religious poetry, one finds the same drama out of which the *Songs and Sonets* arose, the same sense that one is overhearing part of a lively dialogue, in which the speaker, unlike Hamlet's stepfather, may expect to be heard and to be answered: "Thou hast made me, And shall thy worke decay?" ("Holy Sonnet I," l. 1); "If poysonous mineralls, and if that tree,/Whose fruit threw death on else immortall us,/If lecherous goats, if serpents envious/Cannot be damn'd; Alas; why should I bee?" ("Holy Sonnet IX," ll. 1-4).[1]

This confrontation of Donne's speaker with his God in the religious poetry leads into the same kind of argument found in the *Songs and Sonets.* Many of the religious poems are not prayers, nor are they monologues in which the speaker addresses himself to an idea. Contention is paramount in them; whatever else they show about Donne's speaker, they show that his faith was only with difficulty arrived at and that, although he has arrived at what must be seen as a clear and final faith in God and in his own virtue, there are still things to be argued. Whether writing secular or religious poetry, Donne's speaker saw his world in the same way: "Oh, to vex me," he says in "Holy Sonnet XIX,"

> . . . contraryes meet in one:
> Inconstancy unnaturally hath begott
> A constant habit. (ll. 1-3)

This is a statement about the world of the casuist in which "contraryes" are the stuff of life and the only stable element. It is a world in which opposites attract and give each other value: "As humorous is my contritione/As my prophane Love, and as soone forgott" (ll. 5-6). Yet the understanding of that world, a rational understanding derived from experience, an understanding which results in a belief in inconstancy and inconsequence, is shot through with another, different belief: "Those are my best dayes, when I shake with feare" (l. 14). The constancy of the one has very little to do with the constancy of the other. They are discrete. Yet, taken together, they add up to the speaker's concept of his world.

One does not find exactly the same kind of poetry in the religious poems as in the secular. The confrontation of the speaker with the immediate and ultimate values of religion shifts the tone of the poems to high solemnity, and the gay and sometimes frenetic wit is lacking, though the solemn wit in them is akin to that to which the reader has become accustomed. A general characteristic found in much of the religious poetry is the quality of argument. In "Hymne to God my God, in my sicknesse," the pattern is seen:

> . . . As I come
> I tune the Instrument here at the dore,
> And what I must doe then, thinke here before. (ll. 3-5)

The argument is unrestrained by the fact that the speaker of the poem argues with himself; and an understanding of the argument is made easy by the fact that the argument is over "what I must doe then." It is the familiar argument over an action.

The speaker, lying on his bed contemplating death, sees himself going West toward the setting sun and toward death and around the Straits of Magellan. The speaker sees that "this is my South-west discoverie/*Per fretum febris,* by these streights to die" (ll. 9-10). The argument of the poem is between the fact, "theire currants yeeld returne to none" (l. 12), and the deeper fear: "What shall my West hurt me?" (l. 13).

The argument in the poem arises out of the speaker's own recognition of himself, lying there on that bed sick unto death and, like a ship, increasingly disabled but not near its port. The recognition by the speaker of his state is clear: "by these streights to die" (l. 10). It is a knowledge out of the reason that the speaker confronts: he is actually dying. This knowledge is shared by him and the physicians who

> . . . by their lore are growne
> Cosmographers, and I their Mapp, who lie
> Flat on this bed. . . . (ll. 6-8)

Even in this ultimate moment of the speaker's life, he cannot forgo the opportunity to confront varieties of truth. *West* as a direction and as a concept is provable; but the speaker knows that, as he is a Christian, it is the *East* which holds his home: while he goes West in his experience of death, he goes East in his experience of the resurrection. The two truths are the same as those confronted in the works of the casuists: the one a recognition of what joins man to man—the progress toward death and the West; the other that which sepa-

rates and which is derived from processes other than the
reason—the progress toward the East and resurrection.
The remainder of the poem, after the first two lines of
the third stanza, is a process of union of these two
truths:

> . . . as West and East
> In all flatt Maps (and I am one) are one,
> So death doth touch the Resurrection. (ll. 13-15)

It is interesting to note that, like the casuists, the
speaker of the poem, even in his extremity, employs the
same method as the casuists: it is only through the
public and reasonable truth that one comes to under-
stand the private and unreasonable one: "Therfore that
he may raise the Lord throws down" (l. 30).

Donne's metaphors here are similar in their structure
to what one expects in the *Songs and Sonets.* In this
poem the speaker presents his argument in two images,
the first presented in the first stanza, the image of a
person passing through a succession of rooms, in the last
of which he will join the "Quire of Saints" (l. 2) and be
made "thy Musique" (l. 3). The image itself, of the
movement through the rooms by a person who joins in
that last room a choir of persons who have made the
same short journey, is expressive of the same kind of
movement found in Donne's images: as one prepares to
join this choir, one pauses and tunes one's instrument.
The image has been arrived at inductively, and the
speaker employs it to suggest a law of behavior of a class
of persons, musicians. The room is "Holy," the choir
one of "Saints," and the image is a metaphor for the
progression through death to resurrected life. The image
itself, perfectly understandable, is employed as a means
of articulating a nonverbal and nonrational truth: the
preparation for the resurrection. There is tension be-

tween the concept the speaker seeks to define and the articulation of that concept in the image. The tone in these stanzas of *proof*, and, finally, of contention, suggests their near kinship with the poems of the *Songs and Sonets*. The contention of the poem is the obvious one: West opposing and denying the East, death opposing and denying the resurrection; and the speaker resolves that opposition in the manner in which one has come to expect. The private truth is united with the public in such a way as not to deny either; the private is stated in terms of the public: "Therfore that he may raise the Lord throws down" (l. 30). The private truth is made contingent upon an understanding of the public and is stated in terms of it.

The casuistry of this poem suggests that others of the religious poems are informed by the same mode of thought. Consider "Holy Sonnet XIV," where, in a different way, the speaker uses a casuistical argument to deal with a double truth, arriving in the end at a paradoxical conclusion in the manner of the casuists. "Batter my heart," the speaker says in the first line, telling his God to fight him. Anything that needs to be battered offers resistance, and Donne reinforces that sense of resistance in his substitution of *break, blow, burn,* for *knock, breath, shine*. The first quatrain establishes a dichotomy of will in Donne himself, for he not only recognizes that—whatever he is—he resists God, but he also recognizes that he wants that resistance broken down. It is a recognition by Donne in this first quatrain of a double and contradictory truth about himself, and the business of the poem is the reconciliation of that contradiction.

The second quatrain of the sonnet elaborates on the contradiction. Here the speaker is a "usurpt towne" (l. 5), but a split is made between the body of the town and the reason, "your viceroy" (l. 7), which rules it and which proves "weake or untrue" (l. 8). It is the reason which resists God, and it is the body, the town, which would normally and does now seek to accept God. The one, the rational, is exterior; the other, the physical, is interior. The concluding sestet of the poem operates in the way of all casuistry: it states its conclusion in terms of the interior, physical truth, "Yet dearely'I love you, 'and would be loved faine,/But am betroth'd unto your enemie" (ll. 9-10). The sexual imagery, seemingly so out of place in a "holy" sonnet, is there precisely because Donne recognizes the double truth of love, the fact that love is both resistance and attraction. And, when Donne concludes,

> Divorce mee, 'untie, or breake that knot againe,
> Take mee to you, imprison mee, for I
> Except you'enthrall mee, never shall be free,
> Nor ever chast, except you ravish mee (ll. 11-14)

he is stating explicitly that simple acceptance by God of Donne and his errant rationality will not do, for that would be to deny the rationality. Donne cannot be chaste unless he is ravished by God, a rape which, in its nature, is not possible without resistance. By asking for rape, Donne is asking for recognition—he demands it, really—of the powers of both his reason and his physical nature.

It is of the nature of the mind of the casuist that he believe fervently in the powers, however limited, of his reason; and he insists on doing the impossible, for he insists on holding on to an irrational truth while articulating that truth through the reason. Donne asks, in "Batter my heart," to be destroyed. God is faced here with a man, fully man, uniting in himself all the powers of reason and the body and the spirit. Even though willing to enter into the lists with God, even though willing to be beaten, this man knows that the only way he can be joined with God is through battle, no matter how loving. This is orthodox Christianity, and it is orthodox càsuistry, for it recognizes the contrarieties of both the reason and the body, the divine and the human; and, in a peculiar way, it reconciles them.

The conclusions of Donne's poems, whether the poem presents a confrontation with some sleazy woman, Donne's wife, the mistress of his soul, or what must be seen as Donne's serene God, are always paradoxical. Here is the pattern: "Nor ever chast, except you ravish mee" (l. 14). One can see the difference between the paradoxes that end the religious poems and the paradoxes that end the secular poems of the *Songs and Sonets*. The speaker of the religious poems finds himself forced to define paradoxes and to argue toward them for different reasons from those which force the speaker of the *Songs and Sonets*. The speaker of the *Songs and Sonets*, besieged by the very reasonable view of the "you," argues toward a paradoxical view which will assert his own individuality and importance within the structured world. It is an assertion of the primacy of self; as he asserts *we may have sex* or *sloth is fine*, he insists on the importance of the private view. In the religious poems, the speaker, arguing toward the same kind of paradox, finds himself in a relatively different situation. As he is in a religious context, it is the public and external view that is paradoxical. It is the speaker who asserts the reasonable and understandable view. In short, the paradoxes which closed the secular poems assert the speaker's individuality. The paradoxes which close the religious poems assert his communion with God, for these paradoxes are, most of them, the central truths of Christianity; and, as the speaker triumphantly asserts these religious paradoxes as he concludes his poems, he does so in a manner to submerge himself into his belief, not to make more clear the disjunction between himself and his world.

This study has spoken of Donne's secular and religious poetry, yet the division is invidious, for Donne's poetry and his concerns in that poetry are seamless and whole. Donne's poetry, the great mass of it, is secular and worldly, in whatever collection it may be found. In October, 1621, writing to Sir Thomas Lucy, Donne asks, "Why do you say nothing of my 'little book of *Cases*?' " (Gosse, II, 151), indicating fairly late in his life his continued interest in casuistry. The letter indicates what we already know: even in the most spiritual of the religious poetry, the poet is still writing about moral, not ascetic, theology. He remains the pastor, akin to those Jesuits sitting in confessionals passing out judgments and the preachers in the Anglican churches of England who concerned themselves with the virtue of their flock. Of all the religious and of all the religious concerns, the moral theologians were the most worldly, facing their congregations, asking and answering the question *What do I do?* Like the lawyer in Luke's gospel, the poems ask the question, *What good must I do to inherit eternal life?* Donne, following Christ, answers, *Keep the commandments.* Both know that there is the further, heavier responsibility: *Sell all you have and give to the poor. And follow me.* Both know that the first part of the answer leads directly into the second part. Moral theology, even for lawyers, leads directly into ascetic theology, and neither the poet nor his reader need wonder at the poet's stopping this side of that line; his answers lead, like Christ's, into others.

The mind of man need not always be "passing moral judgments." Joseph Hall, a moral theologian, was at other times in his life a satirist with Donne and a preacher with him; and for some time in their middle years and before either man had settled himself, they were both under the patronage of Sir Robert Drury. "Passing moral judgments" is only one activity of the mind of man. Donne's speaker, in the *Songs and Sonets*, is, in his own peculiar fashion, a moral theologian, but insofar as he is Donne himself, he is only one side of Donne. The poet may be a casuist like his speaker, but he may also be a satirist, a preacher, and an intellect under the patronage of the King and Sir Robert Drury. It is important, consequently, to distinguish between the mind of the casuist and the mind of the poet. The speaker, always a doubting conscience, differs from the poet, who, on some occasions, showed no doubt, and, on others, had no need of conscience.

There are of course poems in the collection of the *Songs and Sonets* which are not informed by the casuistical spirit. "Nocturnall upon S. Lucies day," despite the intricacy of its argument, has nothing to do with moral theology. There are others which either are not at all predicated upon a question about an action or else are only minimally predicated upon moral questions. Several of the religious poems seem to be outside this tradition, poems in which the speaker ruminates with himself over a matter, investigating the implications of his concerns. The satires are very little informed by this tradition; they thunder against wrong, but they do not argue about the nature of that wrong, and the speaker shows no doubt. The verse letters, by and large, are investigatory lyrics, and the *Paradoxes and Problems,* though delightful and certainly paradoxical, have more to do with the Renaissance tradition of paradox than with casuistry.

As we compare the varieties of literary expression in

which Donne wrote, poetry and prose, and judge which of those works succeed on their own terms, it is possible to distinguish between the mind of the speaker and the mind of the poet. There appear to be certain characteristics which recur in the works of the poet, qualities of mind which are definable and which seem at once to produce the poetry and to exist in it. There seems to be an epistemological interest in the poet's mind, an awareness of epistemological difficulties exploited to an extravagant degree in virtually all of Donne's works. The speaker is concerned with the conflict among formulations of truth. He seems to delight in the conflict among words: *sin is virtuous, two are one, constancy is inconstant, West is East, death is life.* The conflict among words suggests the larger and more important problem: the nature and the existence of truth. The problem of truth and its formulation apparently is always present for the speaker in any of Donne's works. There is in Donne's works an extraordinary awareness of self, of the speaker's individual personhood. The speaker seems unable to be theoretic in his investigations or disinterested in his judgment. He seems unable to be interested in those matter in which he does not find himself squarely in the center. The poet exhibits an awareness of audience, of one or a mass of others, of the "you" in the *Songs and Sonets,* the persons in the verse letters, his congregation to whom he delivers his sermons. The writer seems most frequently to speak *to* someone, and to draw a kind of energy from that person. There is finally, a strong awareness of occasion. Donne is always intensely aware of his surroundings, of the importance of the moment. Without regard to the intention in a particular poem or work, the speaker's intention seems to arise out of the moment and to address itself to the moment, the real moment—which may of course be only imaginary—but which the speaker posits as real.

As these concerns of Donne's join together and as they reach their fullest expression, they enter into the most successful writings of the poet, into the religious and secular lyrics, the satires, the verse letters, the elegies and the sermons. The poet's literary ability in verse and prose seems dependent largely upon his ability to express in words some union of these concerns. When the occasion is an action and the epistemological confusion arises out of that action, casuistry results; when the occasion, on the other hand, is a church service and the epistemological interest is biblical, the result is a sermon. Across the spectrum of the poet's canon, these concerns seem to find their most perfect expression in the casuistry of the lyrics of the *Songs and Sonets* and in the sermons. The strong sense of occasion in these two modes, the one moral and the other pastoral, enables the speaker and the preacher to give full expression to the abilities of their minds.

The difference between the poems of the *Songs and Sonets* and the sermons is seen immediately—even when they both confront the same issue and employ the same method: in the former, there is a clear equality between the speaker and the person to whom he speaks, an equality which lends a tension to the poems; in the latter, the speaker is not engaged in a dialogue, but in a monologue in which he does not expect response of a verbal order. In the poems, the speaker feels himself an anomaly. In the sermons, by definition, the speaker is preacher and has access to a truth which is public and authoritative. The preacher himself does not doubt.

The kinds of interest the poet exhibits seem to find their most perfect expression in these two modes, and this is so, apparently, because of the strong sense of occasion inherent in both modes of expression. The two modes have in common an epistemological concern and a sense of self, of audience, and of occasion; other forms of expression in the canon of the poet may share with the *Songs and Sonets* and the sermons one or another of these interests, but across the spectrum of the poet's writings there is only a handful of works which succeed and which do not exhibit all these facets of his mind. If there are poems which are not in any way controlled by the moral impulse and yet which are the very greatest art, those achievements are anomalies, eccentric expressions which serve to illuminate the poet's more characteristic thought and method.

More frequently, when the poet's strong sense of epistemological difficulty is not united with a strong sense of occasion, the poems fail. "An Anatomie of the World" and "The Progresse of the Soule" both exhibit a strong epistemological concern, but neither poem is able to make the immediate occasion for that poem identical with or suggestive of that epistemological difficulty. The poems seem *vacant* because the epistemological confusion is not clearly linked to the occasion for that confusion, the death of Elizabeth Drury. Criticism has borne out this judgment, and those critical analyses which have attempted to resolve the epistemological confusion by resort to philosophy and metaphysics have failed. The failure is Donne's, not the critics'. The mode of expression which he has chosen apparently does not suit his particular abilities. And, as the critic searches for *what* it is that Elizabeth Drury represents, he fails precisely because Donne is normally unable to write a philosophical or metaphysical poem. Ben Jonson, in his conversations with William Drummond, says of the poems "That Done's Anniversarie was profane and full of blasphemies: that he [Ben Jonson] told Mr. Done, if it had been written of the Virgin Marie it had been something; to which he answered, that he described the Idea of a Woman, and not as she was" (p. 3). Jonson, here, arrives at the heart of the difficulty of these poems and shows why the poems are finally, with all their interest, beyond the canon of Donne's finest poems. The poet writes his finest poetry when he is confronted with a woman who is more than the "Idea of a Woman," who is a woman "as she was." The poet needs flesh and blood before him. The Anniversaries succeed only in their parts; as wholes they fail because of the peculiar nature of the poet's mind, because he is unable to write in the abstract mode which the death of a girl whom he did not know requires of him. Donne seems unable to write successfully without a strong sense of occasion, a sense he was able to discover in the *Songs and Sonets,* in some religious poems, in the sermons, and in some few other poems. Where the sense of occasion is lacking, the poem generally fails; it becomes merely difficult. And the difficulty of the argument and the elaboration of the investigation strike the reader as being fantastic, unrelated to any reality.[2]

Casuistry is far removed from poetry. The ponderousness of the one seems to have little to do with the cutting brilliance of the other. Poets have always made use of moral dilemmas in their poetry, and it is surely a measure of the greatness of Donne that he was able to transform a method into a poetic. One may assume that, in most of these poems, Bishop Hall and Escobar and their friends would not have recognized themselves. In discovering the frequent similarities between Donne's poems in the *Songs and Sonets* and the casuistry of the seventeenth century, one finds less an influence than a coincidental likeness. Casuistry in all times and places

presupposes the same epistemology and the same meth-
od, and as one assents to any kind of moral structure
external to oneself and independent of the particular
situation, one will need casuistry in the application of
that moral structure. And the prevalence of the casu-
istical argument in the poems is matched by the preva-
lence of casuistry in Donne's time. Isabella, in *Measure
for Measure,* is only one heroine of the drama of the
period who finds herself caught, in the predicament of
the casuists, *between sins.* Donne's time seemed to see
itself that way, which may explain the enormous popu-
larity of books of cases of conscience during the cen-
tury. Men did not know what to do.

Men in the twentieth century do not know what to
do either, and we may respond to Donne's speaker and
to the casuistry of the *Songs and Sonets* for that reason.
But it is clear we should be careful in our response to
the poems. The association made here between the
Songs and Sonets and the method of reasoning called
casuistry has had, in part, a submerged motive, and that
is to dissociate Donne from our own century and even
from some of his admirers in his own. Donne has been
admired for the sudden and sometimes elaborate bril-
liance of his wit, for the daring and determined intricacy
of his argument. His gaiety in the face of men and
women and God, and in the face of a world which is at
most translucent, has been attractive to the twentieth
century whose world seems as murky. We would like to
feel that, facing such a world, we could be as deter-
mined, as daring, and as successful. The twentieth cen-
tury has seen its difficulties mirrored in his.

But our difficulties are not Donne's, and our diffi-
cult response to our world is different from Donne's
difficult response. In many ways the separation is episte-
mological. In the twentieth century, people tend to be

skeptics viewing the world with disinterested amusement or disdain, or scientists investigating inductively the natural phenomena, or protestants relying on a private view of the world, on faith and the individual conscience and experience, or technologists, who believe that method is all. And moralists now assent to situation ethics where *occasion* is paramount and truth does not exist separate from occasion.

But Donne knows that truth exists, that inductive reasoning does not necessarily lead to truth, that the private view is not paramount, and that truth does exist separate from its application. When he says, in "The first Anniversary," "new Philosophy calls all in doubt,/ The Element of fire is quite put out" (ll. 205-6), he is saying in different terms what he says in "Holy Sonnet XVIII":

> Sleepes she a thousand, then peepes up one yeare?
> Is she selfe truth and errs? now new, now outwore?
> Doth she, and did she, and shall she evermore
> On one, on seaven, or on no hill appeare? (ll. 5-8)

This doubt is different from our own, for it is a doubt about the accessibility of truth, not its existence. And Donne's faith in an external truth is of inestimable value, for he may resort in the weakness of his reason to other sources of his truth and he need not be so strong as to stand alone. *All* is not in doubt for him, even though it may seem so at times: he may define his virtue and his sin. We may describe our occasion, but our occasions are discrete and we have no epistemology which will join them. As that is so, we may describe our guilt but not define its cause. We have lost our sense of the "government of things in God," and the world is, for us, in bits and pieces. For this reason we respond to the *difficult* nature of Donne's poems, the sense that they give of strain and dis-ease, the sense of all of the problems of "mans fact," and we forget or ignore the clear statement in the poems of "Gods commande-ment."

In many ways Donne is like us. His conscience doubts like ours, and his mind is as eclectic: he seems to enjoy the same kind of paradox. In doubting he is not bitter, and in believing he is not facile. His temperament is catholic, willing to make allowance for vagaries, for contradictions, for paradox, for disparate plenitude. But Donne differs as he holds onto a hard core of received knowledge, insisting on the possibility of reconciliation between different kinds of knowledge, between differ-ent kinds of men, between men and women, between himself and God. As the poet proves that reconciliation is possible, that *we two* are provably *one,* he shows himself capable of arguing, even in his special circum-stances, from a position of strength, for he is confident that he will arrive at a truth acceptable to himself, the person to whom he speaks, and to God, whose truth it may be. The epistemology and method of the *doubting conscience* have enabled him to do so.

Notes

CHAPTER I

1. R. M. Wenley, writing on casuistry, says that "in the broad ethical sense it indicates rational, and, too often, somewhat empirical analysis of particular problems incident to human conduct." He goes on to say, in a narrow sense, that casuistry presupposes "(a) the existence of external rules, nomistic opinions, or systematic prescriptions (especially the last); and (b) individual cases, peculiar to separate persons at particular times, when approved sanctions seem doubtful or silent, or require elucidation with a view to the justification of exceptions. It deals here with means of action in relation to ends" (II, 240-41).

2. The casuist makes distinctions among various kinds of conscience: a "doubting conscience" for William Ames is one "which yeeldeth to neither part of the question in hand, but sticks and staggers between assent and dissent, not knowing which to doe" (p. 12). Jeremy Taylor's "probable" or thinking conscience "is an imperfect assent to an uncertain proposition, in which one part is indeed clearly and fully chosen, but with an explicit or implicit notice that the contrary is also fairly eligible" (p. 150). Casuistry aims to eliminate this uncertainty: Jeremy Taylor says, "We should have a conscience void of offence both towards God and towards man; that we should be able to separate the vile from the precious, and know what to choose and what to avoid" (p. xi).

3. The foregoing is a "case of conscience," that is, the analysis of a particular "case" in which the conscience is doubtful. Works of casuistry may be concerned with one such case or with hundreds in a dictionary style. A second kind of casuistical work

may be concerned with the total operation of conscience, but these two types tend to shade off into one another. Joseph Hall's *Resolutions and Decisions of Divers Practical Cases of Conscience, in Continuall Use Amongst Men* is an example of the first kind, there being forty cases divided into four types: (1) of profit and traffic, (2) of life and liberty, (3) of piety and religion, (4) of matrimony. Hall says, "These I have selected out of many," and makes no pretense to being inclusive. He does not explain his method; he shows it (Hall, p. 371); the collection runs to 136 pages. On the other hand, Jeremy Taylor's *Ductor Dubitantium* is of the second kind which offers "to the world a general instrument of moral theology, by the rules and measures of which the guides of souls may determine the particulars that shall be brought before them" (pp. xix-xx). William Ames's book is of a more usual type. It is divided into five books, the first of which is definition and general discussion, and the succeeding four are particular cases of conscience: man's duty in general, man's duty to God and to his neighbor. The whole book runs to 427 pages.

4. This concept of law and its place in ethics found its most perfect expression in the *Summa Theologica* of Thomas Aquinas. All the seventeenth-century casuists, Protestant and Catholic alike, build upon Aquinas and define themselves in relation to his work, though there are differences among them as to the uses of reason in discovering law and differences as to the kinds of acceptable formulations of the law.

5. The last two named are the most notable of the Jesuit casuists. Azor's major work is *Institutiones Morales; in quibus universe quaestiones ad conscientiam recte aut prave factorum pertinentes, breviter tractantur* (1616-25). Escobar's major work, *Liber Theologiae Moralis* (1659) is perhaps the most representative of the Jesuitical methods of the seventeenth century. Escobar will figure prominently in the present discussion. Not an innovator nor, apparently, a great thinker, he sees himself as presenting for the reader a compendium of the thoughts of other casuists, and his work is therefore particularly useful for the present discussion. He was the major target in Pascal's *Provincial Letters.*

6. My discussion of casuistry, here and in the following pages, makes no pretense to exhaustive coverage. It is no part of

my aim more than to mention the history of the genre, and the differences that separate the Roman Catholics from the Protestants and that separate writer from writer are here only suggested, not analyzed. Donne's fervor, in his poetry seems Protestant, his approach post-Tridentine, but casuistry is a method of reasoning existing in all times and all countries. Although Donne's relation with Joseph Hall was reasonably intimate, we need not ask whether, in fact, Donne had read any particular writer. Jeremy Taylor, for example, writes a generation after Donne's death, but what he says of casuistry in the *Ductor Dubitantium* is as true of the casuistry of Donne's time as of the late seventeenth century.

Most discussions of casuistry are to be found among writers on religious casuistry. Necessarily, their concerns have more to do with answers at which the casuists arrive than with the assumptions behind this kind of argument or with the structure of the argument. There has never been written a "rhetoric" of casuistry. Among the best discussions of the subject are those by R. M. Wenley and E. M. Dublanchy. A fine full-length treatment of English casuistry is by H. R. McAdoo.

7. This discussion will largely concern itself with the lyrics of the *Songs and Sonets* and the influence of the casuistical method on their themes, structures, methods. It is obvious that the habit of thought, exhibited in this collection, would spill over into other collections of Donne's poems. The element of moral theology which we find in the Divine Poems and in the Letters will be discussed in the last chapter. There has been virtually no critical attention paid to Donne's relations with the casuists, except for brief paragraphs in discussions of his prose to the effect that *Biathanatos* and *Pseudo-Martyr* are, in fact, works of casuistry. The one exception is A. E. Malloch's article, "John Donne and the Casuists." In it is found a discussion of the relations between Donne's two casuistical treatises and the tradition of Roman Catholic casuistry. Nothing at all has been written on Donne's relations with the English casuistry of the seventeenth century. Of Donne's poetry, Malloch says, "Donne's poetry is famous for its simultaneous presentation of person and thing: the direct, compelling rhythms are the voice of person speaking to person; yet on this wave length is carried the analytic language of a spatial, objective world. Donne's interest in casuistry, less well-known, exhibits a similar phenomenon: his passionate concern

for the reality and activity of the human self, and at the same time his intellectual absorption in an external world of law" (p. 76).

CHAPTER II

1. Of the fifty-four complete poems in the *Songs and Sonets*, forty-two are spoken to a more or less identifiable "you." Of these, nine are spoken to someone other than a woman: "The Sunne Rising," "Loves Usury," "The Canonization," "Loves exchange," "The Will," "The Blossome," "The Primrose," "A Jeat Ring sent." "Breake of day" is spoken by a woman to a man. The thirty-three poems to a woman and the nine to other specific listeners seem to form a coherent group of poems, viewed from the perspective of their dramatic contexts, and seem to function similarly: the tired but busy sun in "The Sunne Rising" enters into the poetic construction of the poem in the same way, it seems, that the "you" of "The good-morrow" does. All these poems to an identifiable "you" will be dealt with together.

2. Pierre Legouis, writing in 1928, defines what has become the critical consensus: "In many of the *Songs and Sonets* there are two characters; the second is indeed mute; or rather his words are not written down; but we are enabled to guess how he acts and what he would say if he were granted utterance. The way in which Donne gives us those hints is both very clever and very modern. More important still for us here is the effect produced on the speaking character by the presence of a listening one, whom he tries to persuade and win over. What seemed at first disinterested dialectics, indulged in for truth's sake, or at least as evaporations of wit, sounds quite differently when the reader realizes this dumb presence" (p. 38).

3. The relative weight and agility of the minds of these two persons has posed a problem for critics since Dryden made the point that Donne "perplexes the minds of the fair sex with nice speculations of philosophy." Almost no one anymore believes that the "you" of these poems is perplexed by what the speaker says. Not vexed or perplexed, these women are delighted, and the reader has the great pleasure of watching a mature man speak to a mature woman with whom communication is both possible and necessary.

4. Of the poems addressed to a particular person, there are fifteen in which the listener, the "you," intrudes more or less

decisively during the course of the poem. In addition to "The Prohibition," they are: "The Flea," "The Dreame," "Song (Goe, and catche a falling starre)," "The Canonization," "Lovers infiniteness," "A Valediction: of my name, in the window," "A Valediction: of the booke," "Loves exchange," "A Valediction: of weeping," "The Message," "Witchcraft by a picture," "The Blossome," "A Jeat Ring sent," "The Expiration." In some of these the intrusion is perhaps not verbal; in "Witchcraft" after line seven, it is perhaps only a new flood of "sweet salt teares" that calls forth the second stanza.

5. Included in this group of poems are all those spoken directly to a "you" but in which the "you" does not intrude directly during the course of the poem. The divisions, of course, are impossible to make absolute. What one may see in any one poem as an overt action on the part of the "you," changing the direction of the words the "I" is uttering, another may see as a new insight after one or another stanza on the part of the "I" with no overt action made by the "you." It does not seem to matter whether this or that poem is in this or that group, so long as one recognizes that the presence of the "you" does seem to call forth the statement as we find it in the poem and also, in some at least, to affect the shape of the statement as it changes direction during the course of the poem.

6. The poems of the *Songs and Sonets* have been widely seen to have the accents of argument, and occasionally the argumentative tone the speaker takes has been seen to be a fault, misplaced in love poetry. What is not so often noted is that the speaker of these poems is answering, not initiating, the argument. "Womans constancy," an example, consists primarily of the speaker's suggestions for her half of the argument, which he then wittily and cynically undercuts by agreement. The argumentative tone of these poems, then, is at least partially a result of the situation the speaker finds himself in. One senses that generally the "you" begins the confrontation and that the speaker of the poem is not being simply contentious.

7. None of these twelve poems is addressed to any identifiable person. More importantly, any person who might be seen as being addressed exerts no force on the structure or shape of the poem. They exist as statements. These poems are: "The Triple Foole," "Twicknam garden," "Communitie," "Confined Love,"

"Loves Alchymie," "The Curse," "A nocturnall upon S. Lucies day, Being the shortest day," "Loves diet," "Loves Deitie," "The Dissolution," "The Paradox," "Negative love."

8. Of course, such sonnets as 80 and 86 concerning the rival poet, the perplexing 94, and those suggesting some relationship between the Young Man and the Dark Lady are less conventional, suggestive of a greater realism; apparently, in a manner similar to that of Donne, they proceed out of an incipient drama. This also seems to be true of many of the sonnets to the Dark Lady, in which the confrontation of the speaker and the "you" of the sonnet is more than merely suggested.

9. This continues to confront the relation of Donne and Jonson and Shakespeare to the central tradition of the English lyric as it was written in the sixteenth and early seventeenth centuries. The definition given here is arrived at by considering whether the poem comes out of a consciousness concerned primarily with itself, as in most of Shakespeare and Jonson, or whether it comes out of a consciousness concerned with itself in relation to another. To distinguish in this way the central tradition of the lyric from Donne's practice is of course not to deal with other, equally important matters: the tendency toward mellifluousness in the traditional lyric and Donne's departure from that tendency, the use of certain kinds of images generally avoided by Donne, the assumption of a particular tone which Donne ignores.

CHAPTER III

1. The portions quoted in this discussion have been translated from the Latin by Robert J. Edgeworth.

2. William Perkins gives a minimum definition of *sin*, to which all the moral theologians of the seventeenth century would have given their assent, when he says that it is "an anomy, that is, a want of conformity to the Law of God" (p. 6). *Crime* is synonymous with *sin* when sin is seen from the point of view of moral theology. Sin may of course be approached from different points of view, for example, that of ascetic theology, in which case the emphasis is on aspects other than the forensic.

The casuists distinguish themselves according to the relative emphasis they place upon the forensic nature of sin. The post-Tridentine casuists assume that virtue arises from action only insofar as action is in accordance with law. The English Protestants tend to collapse the distinction between moral and ascetic theology and to assume that *action* may lead not merely to virtue but also to holiness. The chief defect of the post-Tridentine writers, according to the Englishmen, was precisely the emphasis that they placed on the legalistic nature of sin. The Englishmen sought to replace the stress on legalism with an emphasis on holiness and repentance. In the confrontation, in casuistry, of a system of laws with one man's private beliefs about his own situation, the Englishmen placed more emphasis upon the one man's private beliefs. The post-Tridentine casuists emphasized the system of law. Both communions recognized that, at a minimum, the act which is sinful is that act which contravenes law.

3. The relationship between truth and law is explained by Aquinas: "A house is said to be true that fulfills the likeness of the form in the architect's mind; and words are said to be true so far as they are the signs of truth in the intellect. In the same way, natural things are said to be true in so far as they express the likeness of the species that are in the divine mind" (I, 16, 1). In the domain of human action, the idea in God's intellect is the principle of action and is expressed as *law*. Insofar as the human action conforms to that principle of action, it is said to be *true*.

4. For a comprehensive statement on the relation between the skepticism of Donne's secular poetry and Pyrrhonism and the libertine traditions, see Louis I. Bredvold, "The Naturalism of Donne in Relation to Some Renaissance Traditions."

5. Donne is a Protestant, and he adheres to the conventional Protestant views about moral theology. In his letters and in his personal life he adheres to the Protestant *probabiliorism*. That adherence does not at all prevent him from making witty employment, in the poetry, of the jesuitic *probabilism*. As I have said elsewhere, Donne seems always serious; his solemnity changes, however, with his subject. As we see him becoming less solemn, we see him becoming more jesuitical and consequently more closely a *probabilist*.

6. In this paragraph the word "conscience" is used in two different senses. When Perkins refers to the "conscience," he is speaking of man confronted with a moral choice who is at the same time situated within a moral framework of laws to which he

assents. Conscience, in this sense, is the mind of man applying the general law to the particular situation in which he finds himself, in order to discover a rule for action.

But, when one speaks of "his own conscience," one means a private notion of right and wrong, some sort of immediate intuition of what should be done. From this individual conscience comes the minor premise of William Ames's syllogism. The individual conscience in its judgment may disagree with the total working of conscience in that one may think one is acting with rectitude while the law says one is acting sinfully. The individual conscience is given, by these men, an importance equal to that of a system of law.

There is an implicit understanding here that the casuists mistrust the individual conscience though they accept its importance. They are fearful of the consequences of the individualism that could result. The supremacy of the individual conscience should be maintained only if it can be controlled by an external system of law. Therefore the business of casuistry is to place the judgment of the individual conscience within the public system of received law. This approach to the importance of the individual perception of truth is that of the faithful—the kind of man characteristic in the Renaissance and in communities of the faithful since then—who feels the world is structured to an end and who abhors the anarchism of the individual perception of truth. While secondary in importance in casuistry, law is a statement of a structured world, and the supremacy of the individual conscience must include an accommodation to that structured world.

7. Helen Gardner's criticisms of "The Extasie" indicate the poem's connection with casuistry:

The word "argument," I think, holds the clue both to the slight sense of dissatisfaction which Grierson expressed and also to the variety of misinterpretations which the poem has suffered. There is a tone of argument throughout the lovers' speech which is out of keeping with the poem's subject. The essence of any illumination received in ecstasy, if we accept the conception of such illumination being possible, is that it is immediate and not arrived at by the normal processes of ratiocination. In ecstasy the rational faculty is laid aside and in a holy stillness the intellect rests in the contemplation of what is, and in the peace of union. Donne's lovers seem very far from this blissful quiet. Their minds are as active as fleas, hopping from one idea to the next. Although we are told that the two souls speak as one and that we are listening to a "dialogue of one," the tone is that of an ordinary dialogue in which points are being made and objections met. When Donne was inspired by the *Dialoghi d'Amore* to write a poem showing the achievement of union in love, he caught from his source that tone of persuasion which has misled readers. The poem *sounds* as if someone is persuading someone. The defect of "The Ecstasy" is that it is not sufficiently ecstatic. It is rather too much of an "argument about an ecstasy." It suffers from a surfeit of ideas (p. 303-4).

On the contrary, the subject of the poem is not an illumination of ecstasy but rather an argument toward an action; and, if the "poem *sounds* as if someone is persuading someone," that is because someone *is* persuading someone. The speaker of the poem is finally insisting that the ecstasy of the middle section of the poem, which arose out of sensory perception, must now return

> T'affections, and to faculties,
> Which sense may reach and apprehend,
> Else a great Prince in prison lies. (ll. 66-68)

Ecstasy derived from the union of souls is a truncated ecstasy, limited, not the human kind. An ecstasy derived from the union of souls and bodies is what the speaker advocates. "The Extasie" is an argument supporting the position.

8. A full analysis of the images which follow line 49 and of the manner in which they are argued is given in chapter 4 of this study.

9. Much of the critical disagreement on this poem has centered around the question of the extent to which the speaker argues specifically toward a sexual union as he argues toward a return to bodies. I believe that, in the range of possibilities which confront the lovers as they return to bodies, sex is one and only one of many possibilities. The speaker does not, even by implication, argue toward this one choice over any of a number of others. Love may surely be "reveal'd" in any number of ways between this man and this woman—in ways which have nothing to do with sex. One way that love is revealed in the poem is the

poem itself: the speaker, loving her, is willing to argue with her for what he feels is their greater good. A consideration in the poem militates against the speaker's having sexual union specifically and immediately on his mind: "To'our bodies turne wee then, that so/Weake men on love reveal'd may looke" (ll. 69-70). If the return to bodies is a specifically sexual act and if the sexual act is in fact "love reveal'd," the imagined observer's presence is voyeuristic and consequently inexplicable. Further, we know from others of Donne's speakers that when love is contemplated, the speaker has found "the world" to be intrusive: "Busie old foole, unruly Sunne." In "The Extasie," the speaker seems inordinately aware of the world and his awareness does not lead him to hostility. Finally, other poems of the collection show that nowhere does Donne fail to be explicit when he means to suggest sexual union. When sex is on the speaker's mind, the reader knows it without equivocation. Donne is entirely capable of suggesting that the return to bodies is a sexual act without suggesting that the sexual act is a debasement of the ecstasy. One cannot say that Donne is discreet about his intentions because of a fear, at the end of the poem, of verbal coarseness or indelicacy. When Donne wants to be coarse, he can be very much so, and he can, above all others, present the sexual union of two persons in such a way as all other unions and all other human endeavors seem coarse by comparison. One has only to think of the third stanza of "The Canonization." If the poet had wanted a specifically sexual reference here, there would have been one. Since there is none, one must assume he did not intend it.

CHAPTER IV

1. Two great centers of thought on the subject of Donne's metaphors are in Samuel Johnson, in the eighteenth century, and in the twentieth century, in T. S. Eliot. Both men comment upon the range of Donne's experience and the fact that his experience comes from discrete areas of the poet's life: thought, feeling, the law, sex, alchemy, astronomy. The two men divide on the degree to which that experience is assimilated into a seamless whole in the poetry, Johnson unable to see more than a mere "yoking," and Eliot apparently unable to see the disjunction between various areas of Donne's experience as being more than merely verbal. I take here a middle course. It is important to understand that the *heterogeneity* of things (in Johnson's phrase) is for the

speaker of these poems very real, the most disturbing quality of human life. At the same time, it is important to notice that there is no *dissociation* (in Eliot's phrase) of sensibility. The heterogeneity of this world is real, and, as people live in it and are "sublunary lovers," they confront that reality. God is real too, the idea in the mind of God is real, law is real, and people are real. The poet's mind joins all. This paradox is not equivocation, and I do not assert it in order to avoid choosing between Johnson and Eliot. It is a paradox which all the seventeenth-century theologians would have recognized. See T. S. Eliot, "The Metaphysical Poets."

2. Rosamund Tuve, in *Elizabethan and Metaphysical Imagery*, analyzes the effect of logic on the imagery of the period. There is perhaps no more important study of the subject even though she slights the importance of the epistemology of the poet.

3. The aim of law, it will be remembered, is to formulate that which is the "proper act and end" of man (Aquinas, II, 91, 2). In that the law is directive of ultimate ends, and in that the law is apparent and accessible, man may be sure of being brought to heaven if he lives in harmony with the law. Ascetic theology, concerned with spiritual progress and holiness, is united here with the problem of the moral act. In varying degrees, the casuists commented upon here feel that the individual conscience must participate in the final judgment on the moral act. It is an insistence on the importance of the private view; and, as it tends to be a Protestant insistence, one would suppose in this respect Donne is closer to the English casuistry than to the Spanish. Man is not a neuter figure in a system of laws; man is an active participant in a living and constantly changing but ordered world. He must have faith in the rightness of what he is doing before the action itself will, in fact, be legal and virtuous. The conscience, in effect, arrives at a conclusion about an action and, after that fact, places both the conclusion and the act in the legal context. The laws, then, are *confirmatory* of private decision rather than productive of such decisions. The moral act can, of course, be placed within a legal context without the individual who commits that act making any judgment at all. One kills, one accepts the commandment, one receives one's punishment. More ordinarily, the casuists, and particularly the English casuists, insist on the

individual's playing his part. As it happens, according to McAdoo, "It is noteworthy that none of the seventeenth-century writers draws attention to the fact of experience that, in practice, the referring of any given action to the general principle is very often an *arrière-pensée* in the total operation of conscience" (p. 73). In short, the casuists begin with the minor premise and move to the major premise.

CHAPTER VI

1. For analyses of the sonnets from the perspective of meditative literature, see Helen Gardner, *John Donne: The Divine Poems,* and Louis L. Martz, *The Poetry of Meditation: A Study in English Religious Literature of the Seventeenth Century.*

2. For the best example of the critic's attempt to describe what it is Elizabeth Drury represents, see Frank Manley, "Introduction," *John Donne: The Anniversaries.*

Bibliography

Principal Sources

Ames, William. *Conscience with the Power and Cases Thereof, Divided into Five Books.* In *The Workes of the Reverend and Faithful Minister of Christ William Ames.* London: Printed for John Rothwell, 1643.

Aquinas, Thomas. *Summa Theologica.* In *The Basic Writings of Saint Thomas Aquinas.* Edited by Anton C. Pegis. 2 vols. New York: Random House, 1945.

Azor, Juan, *Institutiones Morales; in quibus universe quaestiones ad conscientiam recte aut prave factorum pertinentes, breviter tractantur.* Cologne, 1602.

Castiglione, Baldassare. *The Book of the Courtier.* Translated by Sir Thomas Hoby. London: J. M. Dent & Sons, n.d.

Donne, John. *Biathanatos; Reproduced from the First Edition,* with a Bibliographical Note by J. William Hebel. New York: The Facsimile Text Society, 1930.

_____. *Essays in Divinity.* Edited by Evelyn M. Simpson, Oxford: The Clarendon Press, 1952.

_____. *The Poems of John Donne.* Edited by H. J. C. Grierson. 2 vols. London: Oxford University Press, 1912.

_____. *Pseudo-Martyr.* London: Printed by W. Stansby for W. Burre, 1610.

_____. *The Sermons of John Donne.* Edited by George R. Potter and Evelyn M. Simpson. 10 vols. Berkeley and Los Angeles: University of California Press, 1962.

Eliot, T. S. *The Complete Poems and Plays: 1909-1950.* New York: Harcourt, Brace & World, Inc., 1958.

Escobar y Mendoza, Antonio. *Liber Theologiae Moralis.* Lyons, 1659.

Hall, Joseph. *Resolutions and Decisions of Divers Practical Cases of Conscience, in Continuall Use Amongst Men. In Four Decades.* Vol. VII of *The Works of Joseph Hall, D.D.* Edited by John Downame. 12 vols. Oxford: D. C. Talobys, 1937.

Herrick, Robert. *Poems.* Edited by L. C. Martin. Oxford: Oxford University Press, 1956.

Hooker, Richard. *Of the Laws of Ecclesiastical Polity.* London: J. M. Dent & Sons, 1907.

Johnson, Samuel. "Life of Cowley." In *Lives of the English Poets,* edited by George Birkbeck Hill. 3 vols. Oxford: The Clarendon Press, 1905.

Jonson, Ben. *Ben Jonson.* Edited by C. H. Herford and Percy and Evelyn Simpson. 11 vols. Oxford: The Clarendon Press, 1947.

Marvell, Andrew. *Complete Poetry.* Edited by George de F. Lord. New York: Modern Library, 1968.

de Montaigne, Michael. *Apology for Raymond Sebond,* in *The Complete Works of Montaigne.* Translated by Donald M. Frame. Stanford, California: Stanford University Press, 1958.

Pascal, Blaise. *Pascal: The Provincial Letters.* Translated and with an Introduction by A. J. Krailsheimer. Baltimore: Penguin Books, 1967.

Perkins, William. *The Whole Treatise of the Cases of Conscience.* London: Printed by M. J. L., 1651.

Pickering, Thomas. "Epistle Dedicatorie." In Perkins, William, *The Whole Treatise of the Cases of Conscience.* London: Printed by M. J. L., 1651.

Shakespeare, William. *Shakespeare: The Complete Works.* Edited by G. B. Harrison. New York: Harcourt, Brace & World, Inc., 1968.

Taylor, Jeremy. *Ductor Dubitantium.* Vols. IX and X of *The Whole Works of the Right Reverend Jeremy Taylor, D.D.,* edited by Alexander Taylor. 10 vols. London: Longman, Brown, Green & Longman, 1855.

Additional Sources

Adams, Robert. "Donne and Eliot: Metaphysicals." *Kenyon Review* XVI (Spring, 1954), 278-91.

Archer, Stanley. "Meditation and the Structure of Donne's 'Holy Sonnets.' " *English Literary History* XXVIII (June, 1961), 137-47.

Bald, R. C. *John Donne: A Life.* New York: Oxford University Press, 1970.

Bennett, Joan. "The Love Poetry of John Donne: A Reply to C. S. Lewis." *Seventeenth Century Studies Presented to Sir Herbert Grierson.* Oxford: The Clarendon Press, 1938.

_____. *Five Metaphysical Poets.* Cambridge: Cambridge University Press, 1964.

Brauer, Jerald C. "William Perkins." *Encyclopaedia Britannica,* vol. XVII, 1968.

Bredvold, Louis I. "The Naturalism of Donne in Relation to Some Renaissance Traditions." *Journal of English and Germanic Philology* XXII (October, 1923), 471-502.

_____. "The Religious Thought of Donne in Relation to Medieval and Later Traditions." *Studies in Shakespeare, Milton, and Donne.* New York: The Macmillan Company, 1925.

Clements, Arthur L. "Donne's *Holy Sonnet, XIV.*" *Modern Language Notes* LXXVI (June, 1961), 484-89.

Coffin, Charles M. *John Donne and The New Philosophy.* Columbia University Studies in English and Comparative Literature. New York: Columbia University Press, 1937.

Colie, Rosalie L. *Paradoxia Epidemica.* Princeton, N. J.: Princeton University Press, 1966.

_____. "The Rhetoric of Transcendence: 1. Traditions of Paradox in Renaissance Verse-Epistemologies, 2. John Donne's Anniversary Poems and the Paradoxes of Epistemology." *Philological Quarterly* XLIII (April, 1964), 145-70.

Courthope, W. J. *History of English Poetry.* 6 vols. New York: The Macmillan Company, 1895-1910.

Cunningham, James V. "Logic and the Lyric." *Modern Philology* XI (1954), 33-41.

Deman, Thomas. "Probabilisme." *Dictionnaire de Theologie Catholique,* vol. XIIIA, cols. 437-97. Paris: Letouzey et Ané, 1936.

Drummond, William. *Notes of Ben Jonson's Conversations with William Drummond of Hawthornden.* London: Printed for the Shakespeare Society, 1842.

Dublanchy E. "Cas de Conscience." *Dictionnaire de Theologie Catholique,* vol. IIB, cols. 1815-19. Paris: Letouzey et Ané, 1936.

———. "Casuistique." *Dictionnaire de Theologie Catholique,* vol. IIB, cols. 1859-77. Paris: Letouzey et Ané, 1936.

Eliot, T. S. "The Metaphysical Poets." *Selected Essays.* New York: Harcourt, Brace, & Co., 1932.

Empson, W. "Donne and the Rhetorical Tradition." *Kenyon Review* XI (1949), 571-87.

Fish, Stanley Eugene. *Self-Consuming Artifacts; The Experience of Seventeenth Century Literature.* Berkeley: University of California Press, 1972.

Gardner, Helen. "The Argument about 'The Ecstasy.' " *Elizabethan and Jacobean Studies Presented to Frank Percy Wilson in Honour of His Seventieth Birthday.* Oxford: The Clarendon Press, 1959.

———. *John Donne: The Divine Poems.* Oxford: The Clarendon Press, 1952.

Gazier, Augustin. *Blaise Pascal et Antoine Escobar: Étude historique et critique.* Paris: Honoré et Édouard Champion, 1912.

Gosse, Edmond, *The Life and Letters of John Donne, Dean of St. Paul's.* 2 vols. Gloucester, Mass.: Peter Smith, 1959.

Grierson, H. J. C. "Introduction." *The Poems of John Donne.* Edited by H. J. C. Grierson. 2 vols. London: Oxford University Press. 1912.

de Guibert, Joseph. *The Jesuits: Their Spiritual Doctrine and Practice.* Translated by William J. Young, S.J. Chicago: The Institute of Jesuit Sources in Cooperation with Loyola University Press, 1964.

Hollis, Christopher. *A History of the Jesuits*. London: Weidenfeld and Nicolson, 1968.

Howell, Wilbur Samuel. *Logic and Rhetoric in England 1500-1700*. Princeton, N. J.: Princeton University Press, 1950.

Hughes, Merritt Y. "The Lineage of 'The Extasie.' " *Modern Language Review* XXVII (January, 1932), 1-5.

Janelle, Pierre. *The Catholic Reformation*. Milwaukee: The Bruce Publishing Company, 1949.

Kelly, Kevin T. *Conscience: Dictator or Guide? A Study in Seventeenth-Century English Protestant Moral Theology*. London: Geoffrey Chapman, 1967.

Kermode, Frank. *John Donne*. London: Published for the British Council and the National Book League by Longmans, Green & Co., 1961.

Keynes, Geoffrey L. *A Bibliography of Dr. John Donne*. Cambridge: Cambridge University Press, 1958.

Knights, L. C. "On the Social Background of Metaphysical Poetry." *Scrutiny* XIII (Spring, 1945), 37-51.

Legouis, Pierre. *Donne the Craftsman*. Paris: II. Didier, 1928.

Leishman, J. B. *The Monarch of Wit*. London: Hutchinson, 1951.

McAdoo, H. R. *The Structure of Caroline Moral Theology*. London: Longmans, Green & Co., 1949.

Macklem, Michael. *The Anatomy of the World: Relations Between Natural and Moral Law from Donne to Pope*. Minneapolis: University of Minnesota Press, 1958.

Malloch, A. E. "John Donne and the Casuists." *Studies in English Literature* II (January, 1962), 57-76.

_____. "The Technique and Function of the Renaissance Paradox." *Studies in Philology* LIII (1956), 191-203.

Manley, Frank. "Introduction." *John Donne: The Anniversaries*. Baltimore: The Johns Hopkins Press, 1963.

Martz, Louis L. *The Poetry of Meditation: A Study in English Religious Literature of the Seventeenth Century*. New Haven: Yale University Press, 1954.

Miller, Perry. *The New England Mind: The Seventeenth Century.* Cambridge, Mass.: Harvard University Press, 1967.

Moloney, M. F. *John Donne: His Flight from Medievalism.* Urbana: University of Illinois Press, 1944.

Nelson, Benjamin N. "Casuistry." *Encyclopaedia Britannica,* vol. V, 1968.

O'Connor, D. J. *Aquinas and Natural Law.* London: Macmillan & Co., Ltd., 1967.

Ong, Walter Jackson. "The Province of Rhetoric and Poetic." *Modern Schoolman* XIX (1942), 24-27.

———. *Ramus, Method and the Decay of Dialogue.* Cambridge, Mass.: Harvard University Press, 1958.

———. "Wit and Mystery: A Revaluation in Mediaeval Latin Hymnody." *Speculum* XXII (1947), 310-41.

Ornstein, Robert. "Donne, Montaigne, and Natural Law." *Journal of English and Germanic Philology* LV (1956), 213-29.

Peterson, Douglas L. "John Donne's *Holy Sonnets* and the Anglican Doctrine of Contrition." *Studies in Philology* LVI (July, 1959), 504-18.

Potter, Geórge R. "Donne's Extasie, Contra Legouis." *Philological Quarterly* XV (July, 1936), 247-53.

Pound, Ezra. *The ABC of Reading.* London: Faber & Faber, 1951.

Ramsey, Mary Paton. *Les Doctrines medievales chez Donne, le poete metaphysicien de l'Angleterre.* Oxford: The Clarendon Press, 1917.

Simpson, Evelyn M. "Introduction." *John Donne's Sermons on the Psalms and Gospels.* Edited by Evelyn M. Simpson. Berkeley: University of California Press, 1967.

Stuart, Grace. *Conscience and Reason.* New York: The Macmillan Co., 1951.

Tuve, Rosamund. *Elizabethan and Metaphysical Imagery.* Chicago: University of Chicago Press, 1947.

Webber, Joan. *Contrary Music: The Prose Style of John Donne.* Madison: The University of Wisconsin Press, 1963.

Wenley, R. M. "Casuistry." *Encyclopaedia of Religion and Ethics.* Edited by James Hastings. 12 vols. New York: Charles Scribner's Sons, 1932.

"William Ames." *Encyclopaedia Britannica,* vol. I, 1968.

Index

Ames, William, 7, 53; *Conscience with the Power and Cases Thereof,* 174; on "doubting conscience," 173; on law, 42; on logic, 106; on "mans fact and Gods Commandement," 68, 71, 100; on the governance of the world, 39; on the limitations of moral truth, 117; on the man who lives in sin, 53, 68, 107–8; on the syllogism of casuistry, 68, 107–8, 180; on the uncertainty of moral matters, 129

Aquinas, Thomas: as the basis for the epistemology of Renaissance moral theology, 174; on law, 42, 99; on the aim of law, 42, 43, 56, 183; on the double perception of truth, 67–68; on the governance of the world, 39, 99; on the law and the reason, 45; on the nature of truth, 179; on truth and the reason, 39

Azor, Juan, 7, 106, 117, 174

Bredvold, Louis, 179

Cases of conscience: on advising evil (Escobar), 58; on enslavement of innocent persons (Escobar), 91; on murder (Escobar), 35, 125, 128; on murder (Hall), 35–36; on self-murder (Donne), 53–54; on self-murder (Hall), 53; on starting wars (Escobar), 130–31, 132; on the condemned man (Escobar), 34, 101–2; on the defense of gold sovereigns (Escobar), 35; on the fleeing minister (Perkins), 5–7, 14; on the incontinent Jesuit in habit (Escobar), 58–59, (Pascal) 64, 120; on the man who lives in sin (Ames), 53, 68, 107–8; on the nightrider and the baby (Escobar), 112–13, 120–21, 133; on the shame of pregnancy (Escobar), 58; on the slandered religious (Escobar), 111; on the soldier who fights in unjust wars (Escobar), 34

Casuistry: as a choice between sins, 56–65; carefulness of, 128–30; cases of conscience and, 173; definition of, 4–5, 153 (Wenley), 173; inclusiveness of, 124–30; kinds of, 5,

193